The Child from Birth to Three in Waldorf Education and Child Care

Rainer Patzlaff
Claudia McKeen
Ina von Mackensen
Claudia Grah-Wittich

Translated from the German by Margot M. Saar

Waldorf Early Childhood Association of North America

The Child from Birth to Three in Waldorf Education and Child Care
Second English edition
© 2020 Waldorf Early Childhood Association of North America
285 Hungry Hollow Rd, Spring Valley, NY 10977
845-352-1690
www.waldorfearlychildhood.org
store.waldorfearlychildhood.org

Originally published in German by the Education Research Group
of the German Association of Waldorf Schools, Stuttgart
as *Leitlinien der Waldorfpädagogik für die Kindheit von der Geburt
bis zum dritten Lebensjahr*

Translated from the German by Margot M. Saar

This publication was made possible by a grant from the Waldorf Curriculum Fund.

The text was created by a team of authors. The main author of each section was:
Section A: Rainer Patzlaff; Section B: Claudia McKeen
Section C: Ina von Mackensen; Section D: Claudia Grah-Wittich
German edition editor and final text: Rainer Patzlaff
English edition editor: Susan Howard

Photos: Charlotte Fischer, Annette Bopp, Knut Schmitz, Brigitte Huisinga, Claudia Grah-Wittich
Layout by Lory Widmer, based on the German edition design by TEBITRON GmbH

ISBN 978-1-936849-54-3

All rights reserved. No part of this book may be reproduced in any form without the written permission of the publisher, except for brief quotations embodied in critical reviews and articles.

Contents

Introduction by Susan Howard   5

A   Educational Foundations and Objectives

1. Focusing on the individuality   7
2. Development through metamorphosis   10
3. Salutogenesis and Waldorf education   14
4. The special nature of learning in early childhood   17

B   Supporting Development in Early Childhood

1. Conception, pregnancy and birth   21
2. The first year: achieving uprightness and learning to walk   24
3. The second year: learning to speak   27
4. The third year: I-consciousness and thinking awaken   33
5. The child's invisible helpers   38

C   Early Childhood Education and Care

1. Establishing the relationship—the foundation of early childhood care   40
2. Free movement and independent play   47
3. The environment   52
4. Rhythm and rituals   55

D Conditions for Infant and Toddler Child Care

1. The impulse behind Waldorf early childhood education	57
2. Standards of care for children under the age of three	59
3. Basic and advanced training	60
4. Rooms, furnishings and equipment	61
5. Legal and financial aspects	64
6. Quality assurance and collegial work	65
7. Working with the parents	66
8. Working with physicians, therapists and early childhood development specialists	67
9. Working with kindergarten and school	68
10. Social integration	69
11. Starting a birth-to-three program within an existing institution	69
12. Independent Learning and Relationship Learning	72

Appendix: Quality criteria for day care centers with children under the age of three — 86

English-language Resource List — 91

Bibliography from the German edition — 94

About the Authors — 98

Introduction

The lives of young children and their families have been undergoing great changes in recent years, and in response, many Waldorf educators have developed new approaches to early education and care that go beyond the traditional nursery/kindergarten in order to meet the unique needs of infants and toddlers and their parents.

Since the early 1990s, working groups devoted to this special task have been active internationally. World conferences on the "Dignity of the Young Child," held in Dornach, Switzerland and Järna, Sweden, offered opportunities for courageous and often isolated pioneers of Waldorf birth-to-three child care throughout the world to meet, share their experiences and insights, and find inspiration for their work.

Here in North America, we have witnessed a dramatically changing landscape in our Waldorf early childhood movement in the past decade. Waldorf schools now offer a wide array of programs for children under three, as well as parent-infant, parent-toddler and parent-child classes. And child care programs are being founded in Waldorf school settings, child care centers, and homes.

The educators and caregivers who take up these activities find that special additional training is needed in order to meet the unique needs of infants and toddlers and their parents. This recognition brings us to important questions: How can we deepen our understanding of child development from birth to three? What human qualities and capacities do we need to develop as role models in working with very young children? What kinds of environments are needed? How do we work as supportive partners with parents?

In order to address such questions and provide guidelines and support for this important work, members of the German Birth to Three Working Group and their colleagues have produced this publication. We are very grateful to them for sharing the fruits of their work and providing this valuable resource.

This is the third volume in a series on childhood, health, and education, published by the German Waldorf School Association's Educational Research Center. Volumes I and II—on the education of the child from age three to nine—were translated into English and published in 2007 by AWSNA and WECAN as *Developmental Signatures: Core Values and Practices in Waldorf Education for Children Ages 3 – 9*. We are very pleased to complete the series with this second edition of T*he Child from Birth to Three in Waldorf Education and Child Care*. The second edition includes a new article by Claudia Grah-Wittich, "Independent Learning and Relationship Learning."

We see this little book as an important resource for Waldorf schools and early childhood programs who are extending their work into the birth-to-three realm, as well as for parents and caregivers who are devoted to supporting the development of infants and toddlers out of the insights of Waldorf education and anthroposophy.

—Susan Howard
WECAN Coordinator

A note on the translation

We are grateful to Margot Saar in the UK for translating the German text into English, and to several North American colleagues—especially Kim Lewis and Susan Weber—for help with finding terms that are generally understandable to the North American reader. In Germany, "child care" usually refers to programs for children from birth to three, and children enter the kindergarten at age three. Here in North America, infants and toddlers often attend parent-child classes before entering a nursery or pre-school class at age two-and-a-half to three, or a mixed-age kindergarten at age four.

Because adults who work with children before school entrance offer both education and care, we use the terms "early childhood educator" and "caregiver" almost interchangeably. We hope that you will not find the terms confusing. The pronoun "she" has been used to refer to caregivers for the sake of simplicity, not to exclude male caregivers.

Many of the titles in the bibliography are only available in German and therefore we have compiled an additional list of English language resources on birth to three.

---

[1] Members of the Birth to Three Working Group, "Arbeitskreis Kleinkind," of the Association of Waldorf Kindergartens in Germany who contributed to this publication are Gabriela Claus, Marie-Luise Compani, Claudia Grah-Wittich, Heike Hauptmeier, Brigitte Huisinga, Angelika Knabe, Angela Kranich, Birgitt Lempcke, Ina v. Mackensen, Christiana Pfitzenmeier and Gisela Weigle.

In North America, those with questions about birth-to-three programs are encouraged to contact WECAN at info@waldorfearlychildhood.org. In the UK, contact the Steiner Waldorf Schools Fellowship Early Years Group (SWEYG): www.steinerwaldorf.org.uk.

A. Educational Foundations and Objectives

1. Focusing on the Individuality

The image of the human being as the basis of education

As adults we are never neutral in our approach to children. The way we observe young children as parents or teachers is informed by our image of the human being and of human development. This image is rooted deeply within us and we rarely reflect on it consciously. Often it is an inherent aspect of our religious or cultural background. Over the last centuries public consciousness has come to be increasingly permeated by prevailing scientific and sociological views.

Following the argument of British empiricism (John Locke) that the human being at birth is a blank slate (*tabula rasa*) that will only be written upon by life's experiences, the view spread during the eighteenth century that humans, with all their dispositions, abilities, behaviors and inclinations, are entirely determined by their surroundings. With the emergence of genetics in the nineteenth century the pendulum swung the other way and countless attempts were made to prove that all human traits are a matter of heredity. Heated discussions arose as to whether we are determined by our genes or by our environment. Now, the highly polarized "nature versus nurture" controversy appears to be a thing of the past. Today's models of developmental psychology assume that both factors are equally influential and that child development takes place in the complex interplay of genetic and environmental influences.

More recent discussions have begun to focus on the child's own activity, which is considered to be more than just the result of genes and environment. Children, one now assumes, possess an original, personal will to be active and creative that interacts with, changes, and influences the environment.

To recognize children as autonomous agents means to respect their dignity and rights, independently of any genetic or environmental influences, of health or impairment, of race, gender, color, language, religion, social status or their parents' views of the world. In 1989, the United Nations passed the Convention on the Rights of the Child based on the UN Human Rights Charter that guarantees the inalienable rights of each child on earth. The Convention has been international law since 1990.

The anthroposophical image of the human being

Modern views of the human being broadly coincide with that of anthroposophical spiritual science, which also acknowledges the crucial influence of heredity as well as social, cultural and many other environmental factors on child development. Anthroposophical spiritual science is deeply convinced of the dignity and unalienable rights of each child and of their need for protection. It goes a step further, however, in that it does not just abstractly attribute full human dignity and autonomy to children, but demonstrates what human dignity actually means: in each newborn child we meet a spiritual being who is seeking its way into earthly life, a mature individuality who has experienced many previous earthly incarnations. Before embarking on a particular earthly life, the individuality, helped by higher spiritual entities who stand above human beings, condenses all experiences, achievements, liabilities and talents from former lives into the seed of its individual destiny. Children bring their own destiny into the new life without being consciously aware of it. The adults who receive and accompany the children have the task to pave their way with loving care and respect and help them to find their individual way to adulthood in accordance with decisions made before birth. Whether or not that is possible depends on the intentions and attitudes of the adults whom the child meets and the education they provide.

The pre-earthly life of the individuality

Depending on where children incarnate, they find different geographical and climatic conditions, different ways of life, languages and behaviors, and cultural and religious traditions. Genetically, the ethnic group into which they are born and, within this ethnicity, the parents from whom they come also make an important difference. The complex interplay of all these factors makes for a very special constellation into which newborn children do not simply arrive by mere chance

or as the result of some anonymous fate. These factors are a necessary part of their future lives just as the orchestral score is a necessary part of the symphonic concert. The special genetic and environmental factors belong to the destiny planned out by the individuality before birth.

Anthroposophically speaking, we decide in the spiritual world, before we embark on a new incarnation, what specific historical, cultural, and social conditions we need to find on earth and what kind of body will be the appropriate instrument on which we will be able to play our life's tune. This does not mean that we always seek out the most favorable circumstances. The difficulties and obstacles that we encounter might well be essential for our destiny, in that through our struggling with them we are given the opportunity to develop valuable abilities that will be needed for our further advancement.

Our earthly journey begins "in heaven" when the individuality connects with specially chosen parents at a particular time before entering earthly life through the pathway of conception and birth.

There is plenty of evidence that the events of pre-existence, which are often met today with reservation or rejection, were well known to an earlier humanity. Many parents today have also had direct experience of such events. They speak of how they saw their future children in dreams they had during pregnancy and how the individual traits that they perceived during these dreams were later fully confirmed. Even more remarkable are the reports from women (and sometimes also from men) to whom their children announced even before conception had taken place that they were about to join them. They did not appear as images of embryos or babies but as spiritual beings with a distinctive destiny quality that was later verified. The involvement of the individuality who wants to be born could not be more evident.

Individuality in early childhood

Some results from twin and sibling research seem to contradict the view outlined above at first glance. Everyday observation shows, however, that children are not just the product of parental genes and environmental influences. Even siblings born in close succession, with the same genetic make-up and the same environmental conditions, have their own individual characteristics that manifest during pregnancy, not just in the manner or frequency of their movements but also physiologically in the various, often quite unusual food cravings of the mother.

After birth the differences become even more obvious. The way in which infants replace innate reflex patterns by their own acquired arbitrarily-formed movements carries their individual signature. Right up through the kindergarten phase we observe how children of the same ages, who experience the same stimuli and outer conditions, show individual preferences for particular stimuli and impressions that they imitate while they more or less ignore others. Children also seek out influences in their environment that correspond to their own personal developmental needs. Recent studies, such as the research conducted by the Swiss pediatrician Remo Largo, have also produced convincing evidence of the monumental differences that are possible in the development of infants' motor skills, senses, and speech as well as in their cognitive and psychological maturation. Each child follows his or her own individual path.

2. Development through metamorphosis

Although children have their individual destinies, their development follows a certain fundamental law. Parents and educators need to observe this law to allow the individuality to gradually realize its dispositions and life goals according to its personal destiny. It is the law of gradual transformation (Greek: *metamorphosis*). Since the anthroposophical concept of development is different from the one commonly held today, we will attempt below to describe aspects that will contribute to a fuller understanding.

Linear thinking in education

The concept of development, as commonly applied, refers to a linear process that is subject to the same laws and conditions from beginning to end. Transformation does not enter into it. One result of the linear view is the assumption that young children have the same thought patterns as adults, and therefore need intellectual challenges from an early age. Development according to this view is the growth of one, singular capacity, and therefore basically quantitative in nature.

This concept, whether scientifically valid or not, long ago entered pedagogical practice. Two examples demonstrate this: for decades parents believed they could bring up autonomous individuals by allowing their babies full autonomy ("anti-authoritarian" education, or what we would today call permissive parenting). Although this expectation has been scientifically refuted, the same linear thinking is still propagated in regard to the use of technology. Proponents of linear thinking claim that technological competence can only be achieved if children have extensive experience of it from a very early age.

The pedagogical maxim "the earlier the better," as the logical outcome of this linear thinking, takes on an urgent significance for the many parents who worry about today's economic and financial crises. Driven by a concern that their children might not be sufficiently prepared for the growing competition in professional life, they happily subscribe to the idea that children have to learn very early on what they need to know in later life.

Development in stages of transformation

The behavior described might arise from the best intentions, but it does not correspond to reality. There is only one area where linear thinking is appropriate, and that is the inorganic, mineral realm. Even the tiniest crystal that can only be seen through a microscope is subject to the same law that will apply to all its later developmental stages. There is only quantitative change; no transformation takes place. If we simply transfer this law to the development of living organisms such as plants, animals or humans, we will draw the wrong conclusions, because the development of living organisms does not proceed in a linear way. They are not subject to the same laws from beginning to end, but rather evolve in stages with different laws applying at each stage.

This is an archetypal principle that we can observe in every blossoming plant, which develops in a non-linear way toward the production of flowers and fruit, its ultimate goal. Plants devote themselves to quite different tasks at first when they develop strong roots and stems and lush foliage. Neither in function nor form do they pursue the aim of developing flowers as yet. Only gradually does the plant develop buds and then seeds. Although it is always the same plant that manifests in various forms, it has to pass through very different processes at every stage in order to reach its goal. The achievements of the first stage are subject to different laws than those of the second, third, and further stages.

We can learn three important lessons from this that also apply to human development:

- Each developmental phase has its own "theme" that is entirely different from that of the subsequent phases.
- Each developmental phase creates the foundation for the one that follows.
- Each phase needs its own time. The more time it has to mature, the stronger the foundation becomes for the next developmental phase.

Finding her own way of getting down the steps safely

Polarity and enhancement

Close observation teaches us another lesson, one that we owe to Goethe. He intensively studied plant development and discovered the principle of metamorphosis, which he described in detail in his scientific writings and in his poetry as the law of *polarity and enhancement*. In brief:

The dominant principle during the first phase of plant development is expansion. The foliage grows and expands outward; everything is visible. But expansion does not continue infinitely. After some time the opposite principle, that of contraction and regression, prevails. The leaves get smaller and close up tightly. They form a closed-off space where, invisible to the outside, something new is prepared: the flower. With the bud springing open, the law of expansion once again prevails, although it does not manifest in vegetative growth now but in the diffusion of color and fragrance in the surrounding space and air under the influence of light. Beneath the surface the next stage is being prepared: the greatest possible contraction that culminates in the seed.

From this alternation of opposite principles we can derive a general law: *Development takes place in the field of tension between polarities, in gradual stages of transformation.*

Away from "too much too soon"

If we observe the developing child with an open mind we also discover metamorphosis, and we observe how one developmental stage transforms into its polar opposite. The process begins at birth. After the *lightness* of swimming in the amniotic fluid and the effortlessness of being nurtured through the umbilical cord, newborns are suddenly subject to gravity; they have to breathe, make an effort to take in food and struggle against bodily *heaviness*. They enter a state where entirely different conditions prevail, and they will only be able to cope with the new circumstances if the previous state (that of fetal development) was given sufficient time to mature.

The same applies to the next developmental step. Like the plant in its first stage, young children direct all their energy *to the outside*, to the body, which they learn to build up and control, and to the surrounding world with its sensory impressions. Intense growth and the increasing refinement of organ structures are the theme of this stage. For this growth and refinement to take place children need, next to food, the possibility of experiencing the world through their senses as these perceptions have a structuring and differentiating effect on the entire body.

It is this structuring of the physical organization, especially of motor and sensory functions, that creates a firm foundation for the healthy activity of *soul and spirit* in later life. The outward-directed development prepares the stage that is inward-directed. Children have to be able to *stand* before they can *understand* the world; they have to be able to touch and *grasp* things physically before they can *grasp* them mentally; they must smell and taste things, touch and feel them with their hands in order to experience the world as tangible, comprehensible, and transparent. What appears later as the capacity of thinking is not built up by intellectual understanding, but by "hands-on" activities in early childhood, because these activities have a structuring effect on the inner organs and the brain. The forces that build up and shape the body in early life are later transformed into powers of imagination, thinking and reflection.

If we allow children enough time to follow their natural inner urge for learning and doing and to experience this first fundamental developmental phase intensely, we can trust that the inward-directed metamorphosis from dependence on sensory impressions to the free use of mental activities will occur at the right time for each child.

If parents and educators don't have this trust or knowledge, the maxim "the earlier the better" will lead them to expect accomplishments from young children and infants that only school children or adolescents can manage. It is interesting that little research has as yet been conducted into whether very early formal teaching increases children's performance for years to come or whether it just creates a "flash in the pan" effect.

Waldorf education wants to achieve long-term success. Its maxim is therefore: *Allow children to proceed in their own time. The more time they have to develop fundamental capacities, the stronger they will be.*

Foundations for a healthy life

Anthroposophical education is not only concerned with the metamorphosis of physical processes into mental capacities but also with the reverse, that is, the effect that emotional, mental and spiritual influences in childhood have on the physical constitution in later life. In his lectures to teachers Rudolf Steiner gives many examples that show how misjudged measures of childhood education can manifest decades later in pathological dispositions and how, on the other hand, an education derived from the deeper understanding of the human essence can create a healthy foundation for the whole life.

Knowledge of these long-term effects that work under the surface is as yet little developed, but Rudolf Steiner saw it as an essential tool of responsible educators. The horizon of teachers, Steiner requested, must extend far beyond kindergarten and school. It must include the whole biography—not in order to leave lasting imprints in the children, but to leave them as free as possible, right up to their old age, to continue to learn and develop as individuals because their physical instrument remains intact. Only in this way will children be able to realize the impulses that they brought with them from their time before birth.

Conquering steps

Tasting with all the senses

The practice of education therefore needs to encompass the whole of development from birth until the young adult reaches maturity, and it needs to rest on principles of sustainability and salutogenesis. This fostering of life-long health cannot be achieved with movement and nutrition alone, but needs the physiological and psychological effects of specific educational methods and teaching content. The educator's intimate knowledge of these effects and its practical application will lay the foundations for a lifelong healthy development.

Special destiny paths

What has been described so far applies to "ordinary" healthy development. If lasting physical, emotional, or mental disabilities are present, the educational approach needs to be adjusted. Rudolf Steiner speaks of hidden causes in the destiny structure (karma) of children who are "in need of special care." These causes are not apparent and are not subject to any kind of moral judgment.

Anthroposophical special or curative education does not consider the individuality to be disabled. Body and soul as instruments of the individuality are impaired. With people who are affected in this way the developmental and transformative processes proceed differently: the formative forces that cannot take hold of the organization in the usual way, develop into seeds from which capacities can grow in a later incarnation. For their special development they nevertheless need just as much inspiration, affection, love, and optimal support in this life as "healthy" individuals.

3. Salutogenesis and Waldorf Education

Physical body, life body, and soul body as instruments of the I

Anthroposophy differentiates between the I as the individual's eternal spiritual essence and the three bodies that serve the I as instruments for the realization of its life motifs during its earthly journey: the physical body, the life body that supports all the vital processes until death, and the soul.

In order to be able to serve the I as instruments, these three aspects of the human organization need to be sufficiently developed. This development is a long process that needs careful support from parents and educators—and sometimes also from physicians and therapists—throughout childhood and adolescence until the I first succeeds in penetrating the three parts of the organization. Once this penetration has been effected the young person has reached maturity and no longer needs to be educated by others. Young adults need to educate themselves and take it into their hands to bring their life impulses to fruition.

Education has the task of supporting children while their individuality or I gradually takes hold of the three bodies. This taking hold of the whole human being can also be called incarnation. The adults in charge of education must have thorough knowledge of the laws that apply *in general* to the development of the different aspects of the human organization and their complex interaction. At the same time they need to sharpen their diagnostic eye for *particular* conditions in individual children. Any problems that occur are not seen as personal deficiencies, but as obstacles or challenges in one of the parts of the human organization. The I, as a wholly integral spiritual being, is confronted with these obstacles in its incarnating process.

Salutogenesis as the basis of education

The interaction of the human I with the three parts of the human organization described above is never "routine," either with children or adults. It is a highly sensitive, vulnerable process, and ever-renewed efforts are necessary to establish a healthy balance in the overall organization. That this effort can fail or become temporarily disrupted is an aspect of human freedom. It is also an essential source of illness.

Helping in the garden

It therefore has to be the goal of a true "art of education" (as Rudolf Steiner put it) to help children to stand up to the challenges of this process and to overcome obstacles. When this succeeds we speak of health. Health is not the absence of illness. It is our ability to penetrate all aspects of our organization so that we can realize our full potential in body, soul and spirit. Then we will be free to discover and embark on our own wholly individual journey through life.

Health, if understood in this way, is not naturally given but requires a special foundation that needs to be generated or cultivated through education. Waldorf education here agrees with the findings of modern salutogenesis (a term meaning "origin of health"), where health is not so much seen as conditioned by biological factors but, to a surprising extent, by a certain soul-spiritual conditions that we can bring about ourselves or learn to bring about (Antonovsky 1993, 1997, Schüffel 1998, Grossarth-Maticek 1999).

Salutogenesis research differentiates three areas where certain conditions have to be fulfilled so that an overall state of health can be achieved.

Enjoying a meal together

The ***physical organization*** must learn to deal with foreign substances so that they can be absorbed by the body through metabolism (as happens with food) or be warded off by a healthy immune system. We observe that babies and infants are not born with this ability. It needs to be gradually developed. Salutogenesis attaches particular importance to the fact that the physical body gains strength and learns to assert itself when it struggles to deal with "obstacles."

The ***soul organization*** needs to experience coherence, that is, the feeling of being securely connected with the world. This inner certainty only grows if children unconsciously experience that if the necessary efforts are undertaken, the world in principle a) can be understood, b) can be managed and shaped, and c) is meaningful, so that the child's own efforts make sense and life's challenges are worth tackling.

The ***spiritual organization*** is strengthened by experiences of coherence that give rise to a capacity that is an essential precondition for mastering problems and for gaining courage and inner strength, a capacity that, in salutogenesis, is usually referred to as "resilience" (Opp 1999). Resilient individuals can draw on resources that help them resist the hardships and adversities of life if they do not accept them as an unalterable fate but instead see them as challenges that need to be overcome. Resilience is based on the deeply rooted certainty that our own powers grow if we engage with the world and that obstacles further our development. Feelings of safety, love, trust, and faith, along with reliable human attachments, consolidate this certainty.

The body's ability to assert itself, coherence, and resilience form the foundations that allow us to realize our personal impulses and plans for our lives and to become productive and creative individuals. Autonomy does not, as will be shown, grow from intellectual learning. It arises if children actively engage with the world through all kinds of *primary experiences*, if they learn to master their bodies through free, imaginative play and through dealing with life's challenges—in short, from all self-educative processes that generate healthy (salutogenic) foundations. An education that leaves children free to unfold their individual powers and capacities will consequently need to be profoundly salutogenic.

4. The special nature of learning in early childhood

Education is self-education

The biologist Adolf Portman was not altogether wrong when he said that human beings are born prematurely. Newborns seem entirely helpless and dependent in the first months of their life, which does, however, not make them "blank slates," mere objects waiting to be trained and conditioned. Children come into the world with the essential capacity for self-education. From the very first day children "teach" themselves due to an astounding, ceaseless urge for learning and activity, but also due to their unrestrained openness and devotion to impressions and influences in their environment. Primal trust in the world, in their attachment figures, and in their own powers are the best foundations for children on their way to mastering their bodies and the world.

It is important for this self-educative process that children constantly have the opportunity for primary experiences in the world, that is, experiences gained directly on and through their body. Infants are open to their environment with all their senses, they apply available muscle movements to explore their own body and their surroundings, and they communicate intensely with adults. At the same time they unconsciously incorporate all that they experience into their still-malleable physical constitution, a process that is clearly reflected in the structures of the brain.

Learning in infants therefore happens in the intimate interaction with the physical foundations. All possible physical experiences contribute to it, while learning at the same time shapes and structures the body. Learning at this age is an indirect, implicit process that is not spurred by reflection and intellectual operations but by *activity and perception*. The situation will be quite different later in school.

All mental activities of infants are therefore unconscious and directed to the outside. Completely unselfconsciously, young children explore the world rather than their own selves, which accounts for their enormous and intense learning capacity that will never be achieved again in later life. The learning process consists of total devotion to what can be experienced, and therein lies its universal power. Intellectual judgment and abstraction are foreign to children of this age. Children do not judge; they imitate unquestioningly.

Mastering everyday situations

Learning through bonding

As a result of their intimate ties to sensory perception, children of this age experience everything in relation to particular situations, places, and people. What has been experienced is then committed to memory within this context. Take language, for instance: children experience the words and sentences adults

speak to them in conjunction with gestures and facial expressions, with a particular tone of voice, rhythm or intonation. They experience that these acoustic-visual impressions always go with certain objects or facts, feelings or intentions. Children find this relationship highly interesting and language becomes the means of social bonding, of communication and interaction.

The realities that children experience in adults through the senses gradually unlock for them also the realities of soul and mind. All learning in early childhood consequently depends on the intimate, reliable

attachment to one or more attachment figures. Learning is tied to people; it happens with the help of someone who gives love and affection, who is role-model and inspiration, who offers guidance and sets boundaries.

The child's capacity for self-education is wasted without adults who are willing to give direction and assume responsibility for a healthy development. In contrast to animals, which are led by instincts and whose development is largely predetermined, children come into the world incomplete and undetermined; their further progress wholly depends on the conditions they find. They learn to walk and speak only if there are adults who perform these primal human activities so that they can be imitated.

The inseparable duality of self-education on the one hand and education by the environment on the other is corroborated by modern scientific findings. Brain research has established that humans are the only living creatures who have the freedom to continue to change their brain functions through practicing and learning up to a ripe old age (Eliot 2001, Hüther 2001, 2002, Doidge 2008). Attachment research, on the other hand, shows that people cannot be free and autonomous in later life if they were not able to form an intimate, secure attachment to a primary caregiver in early childhood (Bowlby 1966, Ainsworth 1978, Grossmann & Grossmann 2003), proving that children depend on education and self-education from the moment they are born.

Learning through playing

Children love playing and they need to play. For children playing is not a pastime as it is for adults, but is necessary for their development. Even in the womb babies are engaged in playing with their fingers; they swallow, taste, touch, and turn and in doing so they have the first experience of themselves and their body. After birth, self-experience and experience of the world come together in the playful exploration of motor and sense activities. There is no pressing purpose. The activity of trying out, discovering, and repeating, unconsciously at first, is pure bodily practice. By activating their own will out of a deep inner impulse, by finding out what objects feel like and by observing how these objects respond when a will works on them, children educate themselves.

Parallel to children's gradual development, their way of playing also changes as they grow older. During the first years children play out of a physical urge for activity. It is only at the age of two-and-a-half to three, when the child's sense for subject-object relations awakens, that imaginative play becomes possible.

Learning through imitating
The infant's means of self-education is different from that of adults but much more effective: young children learn by *imitating*.

It is important to know that the anthroposophical concept of imitation is fundamentally different from that of the psychologist Albert Bandura who, in his

Social Learning Theory ("learning through observing models") presents psychological factors such as pleasure and aversion, and strengthening through rewards as incentives for learning. According to Waldorf education the capacity for imitation arises from the special organic-physical situation of young children: their sense activity, which is intensely receptive to all impressions in the environment, takes hold of the body's physiological processes directly and without conscious processing. Much of what happens in the organs is hidden from observation, but if we look closely we can discover the profound organic impact that sense impressions have and how they manifest in the body as symptoms of stress or relaxation. We can observe the immediacy of sense impression and physical response when we see a mother conversing and playing with her baby during diapering: the baby absorbs the adult's motor activity, facial expressions, and gestures, and imitates them.

The child is all sense organ

Enjoying the sense of touch

Of all organ systems it is the neurosensory system that is furthest developed and most fully functional at birth. This is why babies are so open and susceptible to all outside impressions, to the material-substantial world around them with its infinite diversity of touch and warmth sensations, colors, sounds, and smells, and to the language and emotional expressions of their attachment figures. They give themselves wholly to their sense impressions and are not yet able to consciously withdraw from them or observe them critically. What children take in is not processed through thinking and reflection as it will be in later life, but is directly absorbed by the body and its organs.

Learning happens through physical activity and we could therefore also say that the child is all will-being. Because young children are constantly active, taking in and imitating what happens around them, impressions are taken deeply into the unconscious physical processes and imprinted into the structure and function of organs, into growth and form. This means that, in the education of very young children, the material as well as the social and human environment is of paramount importance.

Bodily religion

In their devotion to their surroundings, children experience something like a *bodily religion*. What they take in as gratitude, love, respect, meaningful actions, authenticity, care, and reliability from their caregivers is unconsciously absorbed into the body where—long before such perceptions and experiences can be consciously penetrated—it becomes an unconscious source of safety and primary trust in a higher order. This is where the foundation is laid for the child's moral, religious, emotional, and social education, not through words but through the meaningful actions and moral attitudes of adults. Children absorb them unconsciously and take them deep into their physical organization where they form the foundation for their entire future life.

B. Supporting Development in Early Childhood

1. Conception, Pregnancy, and Birth

Conception

In each newborn child we meet a spiritual entity, an individuality who has passed through many earthly lives before. That this being, who arrives on earth at the moment of birth, has existed long before its physical birth and even before conception took place, can be experienced by many parents who sense the arriving individuality or meet their future child in a dream. In particular, parents with several children often describe how these pre-birth encounters were different with each child. The child's journey from the spiritual to the earthly world can therefore be consciously accompanied much earlier than is generally assumed.

The parents' love for each other offers children the possibility to incarnate, and the more love, selflessness, and joy accompany their reception the healthier the foundation for their future lives will be. With their positive anticipation of the new arrival, parents prepare at the soul level what is prepared physically during conception. A space is provided in the mother's womb where another being can grow that has its own immune system. This is an act of "physical love and selflessness" that we do not find anywhere else in life: the new being is not rejected as foreign tissue, as would normally be the case.

The fertilization and hormonal changes in the mother's organism are not isolated events but form part of a complex network of circumstances. This includes the social environment and the family situation with its worries and conflicts, as well as the relationship of the parents, who might wish for a child or be opposed to the pregnancy and even consider abortion. How parents prepare for the arrival of a child, whether the child is wanted or not, is of existential importance when the indissoluble bond is forged between parent and child that will either nurture or hinder the child's whole future development.

Pregnancy

Modern scientific evidence has confirmed how important the nine months of pregnancy are. The forces at work in the growing child are, however, not visible to us and we have little influence on them. Paternal and maternal genes merely provide a range of *possibilities*. What will develop out of this heritage and the extent to which it will be used is not determined by the genes, but depends on the conditions that prevail in the environment and on the individual child's chosen destiny.

The womb and the maternal organism envelop the child and form its first environment, the first home that offers protection from the outside world. Children nevertheless experience a range of sense impressions and emotional as well as physical influences before birth. These influences will affect the formation and growth of organs and determine how strong the child's health forces will be in later life. Is the mother happily looking forward to her child; is she sick or under stress; does she smoke, drink alcohol, or take drugs? Child development before birth strongly depends on the mother's state of mind and body.

Being pregnant means that the mother has to make changes in her life: she needs to eat more consciously, make sure she gets enough sleep and exercise, and lead a more rhythmic life. The partnership is also affected as is the entire family, their social life and future plans. The mother's mood and emotions, her heartbeat, her voice—they all have a direct influence on the unborn child and its physical development. Again, the joy, love and selfless acceptance that the mother feels for her child will nurture the child's healthy physical development. If there is no joy or love, this has a weakening effect on the child.

In the first two to three weeks of pregnancy the placenta is built up. It is the child's immediate environment and the child plays a vital part in this process. Body tissues and organs are formed, and after four to eight weeks the physical foundation is complete. At this stage the mother might not even have noticed yet that she is pregnant.

The embryonic organs assume their tasks as soon as they are formed. In other words, physical organs fulfill their function while they are still growing and maturing. Formation and function are inseparable, and an intense learning process takes place from the very beginning.

On the other hand, organ growth and physical functions are completely dependent on the physical, emotional, and spiritual environment that the mother provides for the child. The entire development takes place in the intimate dialog between the maternal organism and the unborn child.

From the child's first noticeable movements in the fourth to fifth month the relationship between mother and child becomes ever more real. Children at this stage reveal their own characters in the intensity and dynamics of their movements and in their expressions of life.

When the birth is imminent the mood of reception and expectation reaches its climax. Then we see the child in front of us, but the question "Who are you?" will remain unanswered for a long time.

Birth

The birth is an existential crisis for both mother and child. Recent research has shown that the child's hormones play a part in initiating labor. It is the child's way of expressing the wish to be born. In a process that is painful and exhausting the mother separates from the being with whom she formed a physical unity for nine months. The child moves through the birth canal and starts life on earth with a first cry that signifies the radical change of environment. The confined, cozy, 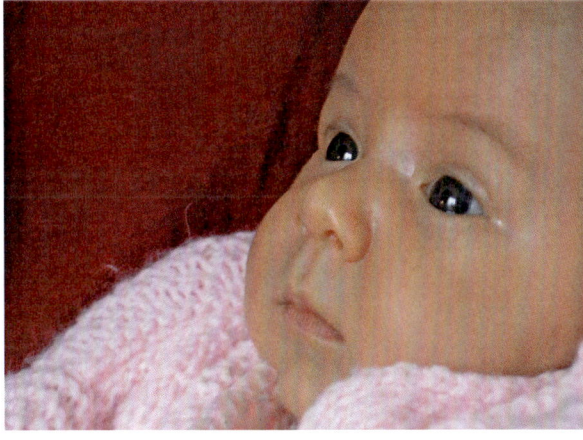 dark, muffled, watery-warm, spherical-cosmic ambiance of the womb is left behind. Breathing, nourishment, elimination, and regulation transfer from the periphery to the center. From one moment to the next sense impressions become intense and new, the lungs have to breathe air, and heart and circulation are separated from the placenta that used to be organ of both respiration and of nutrition.

This separation and finding oneself in an as-yet unknown world can be similar to the experience of death, which involves the transition from earthly to spiritual existence. And just as each death has its own unique signature, no two births are the same. The birth process and its timing and duration form an expression of the individuality. They often characterize the person's entire future path, an aspect that needs to be considered when one decides between spontaneous birth or cesarean section, medical induction and birth delay, when there is no medical necessity. We know today how highly important it is for the bonding of mother and child and for their future relationship that they can stay together after birth and that the child can be breastfed. We also know how important it can be for fathers to be present at the birth. What is often overlooked, however, is that newborn children need to get used to the conditions on earth, to breathing, eating, and digestion, to manifold unfamiliar experiences and impressions, and that this process needs a great deal of time and care. We can only support a child's development effectively if we pay careful attention to his or her individual needs. The child's stage of maturity and own activities will indicate to us what is and what is not beneficial in a given situation.

What happened before birth was strongly influenced by the individuality's will to incarnate. After birth the impulse for learning and development similarly has to come from the child. If we pay careful attention to each child's own pace of entering earthly life, we will be able to accompany and support children in the right way on their individual journeys.

THE CHILD FROM BIRTH TO THREE

2. The first year: achieving uprightness and learning to walk

Toward uprightness

Children acquire the three most important and fundamental human faculties in the first three years of their life when they learn to walk, talk, and think. The fact that we discuss these abilities under three different headings does not indicate that they evolve consecutively. All three capacities are intimately interwoven and develop from the beginning, although children first learn to stand up and walk, at around the end of the first year.

The capacity for speech and language is prepared in the womb and is based on the hearing capacity that emerges very early. A first sound is produced with the newborn's cry at birth, but further speech development relies on the control of gross motor skills that comes with achieving uprightness and the development of the speech organs. In the course of the second year, children manage to articulate first words and sentences, which is still only the basic foundation on which the following years can and must build.

Alongside the capacities of walking and talking, that of thinking evolves. Thinking only finds the foundation it needs in the third year when the first memories are formed, based on the newly arising dualism of I and world. *Conscious* reflection and thought operations will gradually develop on the basis of this foundation, but it is only at the age of about eleven that abstract logical thinking will begin. The same developmental stream produces, one after the other, three capacities that we want to study in more detail.

From reflex to autonomous movement

Children are born with a range of involuntary reflexes such as the sucking and grasping reflexes. They are part of the "basic equipment" nature provides for us. During early childhood these reflexes lose their significance, which is a necessary process since children invest a lot of energy in building up voluntary motor skills and in working on entirely new movement patterns that will eventually replace the reflexes.

The infant's first and foremost object is to gain control over the body in a process that starts with the head, the organ that is furthest developed at birth, and proceeds through arms and hands, the stem, down to the legs and feet.

Control of both eyes, the lifting of the head, and grasping with the hands are the first, still very gentle steps on the journey. Soon children try to change position by rolling over, crawling, and sitting up.

Although the goal of this continued practicing is the same for all children—to stand up and walk—comparative observation shows that the duration and sequence of the various phases, and the intensity with which one movement is practiced while others are passed over more swiftly, differ from one child to the next. The process the adult observes is unique for each child, since it does not represent a law of nature, but rather the personal struggle of the individuality to take hold of the body and overcome gravity, until the first milestone of the arrival on earth is achieved and the child can stand freely with both feet on the ground. Keeping the balance in the face of outside forces, the archetypal expression of human freedom, is realized for the very first time.

The next developmental phase can begin: children now quickly learn to walk. The strenuous conquest of the own body is followed by the joyful conquest of the surroundings, where the toddler now runs around tirelessly and explores every part of it. Whatever toddlers can reach with their hands will be investigated with all the senses and played with. The world with its thousands of objects is open to them as long as no obstacles get in the way.

The formative effect of achieving uprightness

Achieving uprightness is as essential a step in the individual human biography as it was in the evolution of humankind, since it is a necessary physiological precondition for the capacity that sets us apart from animals: the capacity of speech. Speaking, in turn, is the foundation for the development of thinking.

Learning to judge heights

In the development of an organism, just as in evolution, the process of achieving uprightness affects the entire human body, transforming it right into brain and bone structures, muscle functions and organ development. The arch of the foot develops, back muscles and skeleton change their structure, the hands are freed for fine motor skills. The physical foundation of freedom has been attained.

The importance of role-models for achieving uprightness

Although the human body is physiologically designed to become upright, the process does not happen by itself. It needs a monumental effort. Gradually infants have to acquire new skills before they are finally able to walk. This process is only possible, however, if there are people around them who stand upright

and walk. Without their example, infants would never stand up. Their inspiration for achieving uprightness comes from their own individuality, from the unconscious I, but it needs the example of the conscious adult I who masters gravity. The spark jumps from I to I.

How we as adults express our uprightness is also significant for children. The way we move, whether it is hectic and thoughtless or firm, considerate, and graceful, is imprinted into the young child's growing physical body just as our inner uprightness or untruthfulness, our "steadfastness" or lack of it are imprinted into the child's developing soul. An upright character in adults strengthens the child's religious feeling that the world is good.

With our guidance and support infants also take the next developmental steps over the following years: they become more secure in their walking, learn to climb stairs, jump, skip, run, climb, turn around, dance and balance. Fine motor skills also need to be stimulated in the right way by the adult example.

The moral implications of uprightness for later life

How fast and how independently children learn to walk will affect their later biography right into adulthood. We cannot learn to stand and walk without activating our sense of balance, for example, and everything that is practiced physically in this process will later become a soul quality. The ability to aim more and more accurately at objects with hands and eyes due to the increasing control of the eye muscles is the foundation for later intellectual understanding and "grasping."

Standing on the earth fosters a feeling of deep inner trust in children. They experience that the earth carries them and this awakens in them a sense of security in life. It is essential, however, that we do not put a passive child into an upright position. We need to allow children to achieve uprightness by themselves. In this way the child's original trust in his or her own powers is strengthened, which is the basis for all future learning.

3. The second year: learning to speak

Uprightness is necessary for speech

When children learn to walk in the first year they sever the physical body's natural ties to gravity. The body can now become the instrument of free, will-inspired actions in the world. It is no longer restricted to the task of keeping alive or tied to a particular place on earth, but has become free for other, specifically human purposes. The individual can now move freely in the world and pursue freely chosen goals.

In the second crucial stage of child development children learn to free certain physical organs from their naturally determined purpose and make them the instruments for the expression of mental impulses through speech.

At a physical level speech is based on the modulation of the air that streams out when we exhale. As long as the respiratory organism is tied to quadruped locomotion, as in the case of animals, there is not much scope for vocal modulation. For speech to be physically possible we need to be able to control exhalation at will and vary air pressure and volume. In evolutionary terms this means that the freeing of the anterior extremities (the arms and hands) in the process of achieving uprightness is an essential biological precondition for speech development. We can therefore only learn to speak if we can place the respiratory muscles, independently of their natural purpose (which is sustaining life by inhaling oxygen and eliminating toxic waste products) into the service of a higher purpose. Having conquered physical space through upright walking, the child now learns to move freely in the social space, the soul realm, through communication and verbal interaction with others.

From a natural process to the autonomous use of an instrument

Breathing out in itself does not produce speech sounds. The air flow has to be led through the narrow larynx, the glottis and vocal cords, to be made to resound. As with breathing, children learn to control certain muscles, beginning with the first cry and continuing with the gradual development of differentiated sounds and pitches. Crying can also strengthen and exercise the laryngeal muscles.

Sound production in the larynx alone is not yet speech, however. An important third step is needed, which takes place after the air leaves the larynx, when the resounding air escapes through windpipe, posterior and anterior oral cavity, teeth and lips. In this "channel" that is surrounded by muscles, articulation (that is, the formation of characteristic, distinguishable sounds) takes place involving highly complex and fast muscle movements, especially of the tongue. Again, the child needs to free organs from their natural purpose (in this case the chewing, tasting, and swallowing of food) and use them for a higher purpose.

Passive and active language acquisition

Language development does not start with the articulation of first words and sentences but with the very first cry. We differentiate between active and passive language learning. Recent scientific findings show that passive language acquisition begins in the womb. The fetus recognizes the mother's voice and there is clear evidence that newborn children distinguish the sound of their mother tongue from that of other languages. Children also begin to understand spoken utterances very early, long before they can speak words and sentences.

From universal sounds to the mother tongue

Between the first cry and the first clearly articulated words lies a long stretch of time during which children prepare themselves for the highly complex art of sound production by practicing gurgling and babbling noises. Babies play with their speech organs and try out what can be done as one would do with a new instrument. Scientists have established that in their first months, infants have the potential to form the sounds of all languages under the sun no matter where they are, whatever the color of their skin and the milieu in which they grow up. This astounding universality, which also applies to children who are born deaf, is an early indication of the possibility of freedom from natural ties, a freedom that needs to be acquired.

But the road does not lead directly to freedom. It even seems to do the opposite by leading to very close attachment. At the age of about eight to ten months infants begin to become fixated on their ambient language. The ability to produce universal sounds disappears and children actively copy the sounds and speech structures that belong to their environment: they learn to speak their mother tongue.
In order to understand why this attachment to the ambient language is necessary and meaningful we need to know how deeply language learning affects the structures not just of the brain but of all organs, even the blood. This structuring activity generates a clear order that allows the incarnating soul-spirit being to arrive

in the body, which still needs shaping, and use it as its instrument for settling firmly into the world.

Growing up with more than one language

How much children rely on this distinct, security-providing structure has been shown by surprising results from brain research, proving that even if two languages are constantly spoken in a family, only one language center develops in the infant's brain. A second language center only forms in the brain when an additional language appears in the child's surroundings after the child's third year.

This does not mean that we should speak to children in different languages, let alone mix languages, since that would certainly be detrimental to the language acquisition process. If there are several languages in the family *the best rule is for each attachment figure to consistently speak his or her own mother tongue with children under the age of three*. This helps them to relate the language to a particular person: the language is personified, as it were, forming a cosmos of its own. One person's cosmos can coexist as a reliable and safe reality next to the equally authentic and reliable language cosmos of the other person. In this way we create clear structures in the child's understanding of the world and of relationships and avoid unnecessary problems.

When the adults in the family speak among themselves they can use different languages, but not if they address the child directly. The attachment figure with the less dominant language might well be disappointed, as the child, who will soon enough understand the secondary language perfectly, will generally refuse to speak it, a phenomenon that can be observed up to kindergarten age.

This is indeed a positive sign, since children instinctively, and for good reason, strive to find roots in the language that belongs to the place on earth where they have decided to embark on their journey through life. Only when we come in a special way to feel really at home somewhere can we then leave our specialization behind and develop in a new direction, becoming world citizens who are open to the wide variety of languages and cultures.

Learning to speak through imitation

Like standing up, speaking cannot be learned without an adult example. Moreover, the child's capacity of speech and language will not exceed that of the role-model.

The quality of the language that surrounds children is therefore truly formative, in the positive as well as the negative sense. Children do not only absorb what is directly addressed to them. They take in everything that is said around them, the language that accompanies adults' actions, how they communicate and express spontaneous feelings. Children listen intensely and live themselves into the language. We do not need to teach them, we just need to speak. By imitation children take in the whole cosmos of a language—its characteristic sounds, intonation, rhythmical structures, and grammatical and syntactic rules. Children educate themselves by absorbing the language around them. In other words, learning to speak should happen "unintentionally," at the child's own pace, without curriculum, extra practice, corrections, ready-made concepts, or coaching. All we have to do as adults is speak "well," clearly and intelligibly, and above all in whole sentences. Children need a structured order around them to develop structure within.

Media cannot replace "live" role models

For some decades now the misconception has been gaining ground that devices such as televisions and CD-players can promote language acquisition in children, since the language they hear in this way is thought to be superior to the often rudimentary, negligent, or even incorrect language usage of family members. But there are reliable research results that prove the opposite. Language from loudspeakers does not enhance but hinders the acquisition of fundamental language structures, for obvious reasons.

The arduous transformation of the naturally given organs into a useful instrument for speaking requires a real, perceptible I- and will-effort from young children. This effort cannot be stimulated by a lifeless mechanical device. The inspiring spark needs to come from the I of an adult who devotes loving attention to the child. We have to fully focus on the child, in thoughts and feelings, and speak to him or her out of this impulse. Electronic media cannot convey the willed intention to speak. This needs to come from living human beings. Every little story that parents tell, every song they sing, is therefore infinitely more valuable for children than the most perfect presentations from a CD, television, or educational computer software.

Fostering language acquisition

In order to develop in a healthy way children need the "spark" and impulse of being spoken to on a regular basis. It is not the number of words that matters, but certain qualities that ask a lot of today's adults. We must not chatter to children while thinking of something entirely different, but make the effort to keep everything else from our minds when we speak to them. All our powers of feeling and empathy must be involved when we surround the children with conscious awareness. Then, and only then, will our words be true, authentic expressions of our I.

Children need good, structured, versatile language around them to enhance their linguistic development. They do not need copious, intellectual explanations based on abstract thought processes but simple statements that are imbued with warmth and heart forces. Adults should not lapse into "baby-language" since that amounts to caricaturing. It is not genuine and therefore does not help the child. Children relish all kinds of rhythmical verses and nursery rhymes, finger and touching games.

The more genuine soul forces live in our language the better it is for children. Dialects, if they belong to the mother tongue, are therefore real soul food for children. The humor, authenticity, onomatopoeia and immediacy of feeling that lives in dialects have long disappeared from the more intellectual standard language.

The musical quality of language

Due to the linear thinking described earlier we tend to assume that children think and understand language in the same way as adults. But while when adults read or hear something written or spoken in a language they know, they immediately look for the meaning of the words to extract the information they convey, it is quite different with young children. Scientists have recently discovered that while still in the womb babies already listen out for the musical elements of language: volume, intonation of words and sentences, rhythm, tone of voice, nuances of sounds and phonemes, and so on. If we listen carefully to the spoken word, we will find that the elements mentioned hold a message independently of any intellectual content. They carry information about the speaker's mood, emotions, and will intentions. Based on these expressions of soul life children learn to understand the meaning of words. They experience that the words and sentences we speak to them come with certain gestures and face expressions, a particular tone of voice, rhythm, and intonation and that these combinations of visual and acoustic nuances always relate to particular objects, facts, feelings or intentions. Children explore these relations intensely and, in doing so, they experience the connection of language and reality, including the inner reality of the beloved attachment figure. Language becomes a means of social attachment, of communication and interaction.

The power of rhythm

Language, like music, has rhythm. In a spoken sentence we often rely on its rhythm to understand the meaning. Take the sentence "The teacher says the pupil is an ass." The meaning depends on where the speaker pauses and which words are emphasized. "The teacher, says the pupil,

Who wants to join in the morning song?

is an ass" would have the opposite meaning.

Young children bring with them the ability to listen intensely to the rhythm of language. It is of such fundamental importance for their speech development that modern research sees children's capacity for rhythmic differentiation as indicative of their linguistic competence. Scientists claim that if children at school entry age can reliably recognize speech rhythms and reproduce them, then we can assume they can also grasp the inner structure of sentences and more subtle semantic differences. The capacities for rhythmic differentiation and linguistic competence are mutually dependent. According to pediatric audiologist Helmut Breuer the crucial phase for developing the capacity of rhythmic differentiation starts in the womb and ends at the age of three to four, by which time it should be firmly established.

Children do not need abstract speech exercises to support this development; the musical and poetic treasures that have always been used with children are ideal. Every song, rhyme, or verse is carried by rhythm, and helps to develop the children's capacity for rhythmic differentiation naturally. They learn to speak and sing as part of the process.

Other competences are established at the same time. By absorbing language structures through music and rhythm, children begin to practice *thought* structures that, from about the third year, become increasingly conscious. Language prepares thinking, but thinking can only develop on the basis of memory, and memory is strengthened by rhythm. Children love joining in with speech and music rhythms by singing and moving along and, in doing so, they effortlessly learn melodies and words by heart. Due to their rhythm and music, verses, rhymes, and songs become lasting memory treasures long before their meaning is understood.

Up to school age children retain a keen enthusiasm for rhythmic moving games, for words that have a beautiful or special sound, for funny rhymes and striking images. They love being creative with language themselves. Only with the beginning of puberty does this artistic-musical relationship to language fade, giving way to the intellectual penetration of language that is second nature to adults.

If school children are still so receptive to the musicality of language, how much more must this apply to infants and toddlers! These little ones learn to understand language by observing the soul gestures of adults that come to expression in the audible *musical* movements of language and in the visible *spatial* movements of the body, of facial expressions and gestures. It is not by chance that the triad of speech, movement, and music has proved to be the most effective means of fostering language development in children and has even found its place in therapy.

The ethical-moral implications of learning to speak for later life

The more artistic the language that young children are exposed to and that they are able to absorb, the more diverse its vocabulary and grammar, the greater the potential for varied and differentiated perception and cognition that will unfold in adolescence and adulthood when the capacity for thinking, judging, and understanding the world has fully awakened. The more authenticity lives in the words and actions of adults and is absorbed by young children, the stronger will be their sense of truth and their readiness to stand up for what is true when they are older.

4. The third year: I-consciousness and thinking awaken

Thinking in early childhood does not arise, as adults today assume, from mental efforts, rational operations, and reflection but from the intense practice of motor and sensory activities. For several years young children use all their senses and physical abilities to explore their environment. It is the only way in which they can learn to comprehend what is going on in the world and deal with their experiences in an "intelligent" way.

Intellectual abstraction and memorization depend on our ability to dissociate and distance ourselves from sense perceptions, a process that is entirely foreign to very young children. Their unlimited aptitude for learning is not based on distance but on their utter devotion to the world with its manifold events and impressions. To see this devotion as passively absorbing the world would be a misconception. It is in fact the highest degree of active involvement in the world.

Imitation as the foundation for thinking

The special disposition of infants for imitation dominates the first years and remains effective, to a decreasing extent, until about the age of nine. Infants do not just observe and register sense impressions; what they perceive "shoots" straight into the will and is imitated—not afterwards but simultaneously. Young children want to carry out the same activities they see an adult perform, at the same time, with the same gestures and the same objects that the adult is using.

Exploring sizes, shapes, and contents

That this is not idle, childish play but the practicing of the body's unconscious intelligence has been accepted as scientific fact since Piaget referred to the first fundamental form of intelligent activity as *sensorimotor intelligence*. What he meant was the immediate synchrony of perceptions and motor activity that infants achieve without the intermediary use of mental images or rational insights. We could also call it physical intelligence, because the perceptions become physical activity without any thinking taking place. Infants literally incorporate or embody their sense perceptions.

This sensorimotor activity is also important for language acquisition: infants experiment with and try to reproduce sounds they hear long before they can understand their meaning. Content only becomes significant at a later stage of infant development.

Children perceive not only the material world but particularly the people around them. They take in their idiosyncrasies, their way of dealing and talking with one another, their attitudes and so forth. They deeply absorb manners and habits, even a first form of morality. A more intimate relationship is hardly imaginable.

Language acquisition and cognitive development

In learning to speak in their second year, toddlers lay an important foundation for the development of conscious thinking. Recent research has revealed that toddlers not only begin to categorize, they also learn to master the syntax and grammar of their ambient language surprisingly early. They do not, however, take in linguistic structures and rules as consciously as they will do later when they learn foreign languages at school. Language learning for them is rather a by-product of their intense listening and constant practicing. From unconsciously practicing sensory and motor skills children move on to the still-unconscious absorbing of linguistic structures and from there to the increasingly conscious thinking that uses language as its tool.

The development of memory and thinking

As a further essential basis for learning to think, memory skills need to be gradually built up. They range from the young child's recognition of attachment figures to the will-directed inner production of memories that emerge at the time of school entrance. At the age of six to eight weeks, babies recognize their mother or father's faces and smile at them. Memorization gradually increases in the course of the first year and at about the age of eight months infants instantly distinguish familiar from unfamiliar faces. They become shy of strangers and begin to reject them.

At about the same time a new capacity develops. Piaget called it "object permanence": children realize that objects continue to exist even if they can no longer see them. They understand that objects can be hidden and they love looking for and rediscovering them. Up to this stage, any object that was hidden from their view no longer existed. Now, hiding a doll under a cushion and pulling the cushion away again to make sure it is still there becomes a favorite game. Infants can play it by themselves but they prefer if somebody does it with them while they increasingly take the initiative.

With the next steps of memory development we need to consider that young children have a different relationship to time and space from adults. Because they are one with the surrounding sense-perceptible world, they live wholly in the present. They cannot withdraw from what they see or hear to an inner space in order to think about past or future implications. They are fully in the here and now, with their whole being. Children under the age of three live in the present moment; past and future do not yet exist for them.

The capacity that enables young children to form inner representations of outwardly perceived things and processes evolves only gradually, and these representations remain firmly attached to the places and circumstances with which they were originally connected. This means that memorized images cannot be "re-called" at will, whenever and wherever. They only come back when the corresponding objects reappear. It is therefore possible that very young children, once they are back home, have no memory of what and with whom they played at day care, but it comes back to them the moment they get back there. The memory of infants and toddlers is tied to places and we need not worry if that state continues for another few years.

The emergence of this "local memory" does not indicate that free memory forces are available now. It rather indicates that an important first step has been made toward the development of thinking. The capacity of thinking needs to be supported by inner images that are available independently of outer circumstances before present events can be logically linked to memorized events. The child's dissociation from sense perception begins when the local memory emerges, and it proceeds in small steps until about the age of eleven, when puberty sets in and the stage is reached that characterizes adult thinking.

Peek-a-boo!

Playing as an expression of the developing thinking

Infant "thinking" begins with activity. By imitating what they experience at home, for instance, children enter immediately and unconsciously into the logical purposefulness that characterizes everyday activities. Because they keep imitating these activities children gradually learn to understand their meaning. One-year-olds will roughly imitate the movements adults perform with a dustpan and brush. They are content with waving the brush on the floor. A year later they will have understood the purpose of sweeping, due to repeated observation and imitation, and they will begin to move the brush so that the dust ends up in a heap that can then be swept up.

Due to these kinds of experiences, the thinking that gradually emerges during the kindergarten years will no longer depend on sense impressions. Children practice this thinking by playing imaginatively, inspired by ideas and inner images. Once they begin to play "pretend" games an important milestone has been reached: they take up an object and, based on memory, they use it as part of a reality that is familiar to them but that is, at this moment, just imagined. They create imaginary situations that are based on intentional and conscious simulation.

At the age of only sixteen to twenty months infants are able to join in with the "make-believe" games of older children. They will go along with "eating" the cake that was produced in the sandpit, for instance. The child has experienced the real event and the imaginary event centers around a visible representation that is treated as if it were real. As they grow up children develop more and more ideas for playing. They like to pretend to be an adult—the father, for instance—and love being perceived in this role. These are the tender beginnings of role play and they signify an enormously important step in the development of thinking. The fact that children consciously become somebody else through imitation means that they experience themselves as separate from that person. They recognize their individuality and it is this separation of I and world that is necessary for thinking to become detached from the sense-perceptible outer reality, in other words, for thinking to become abstract.

Thinking awakens

Now, in the third year, the third phase in the development of thinking begins when children gain an understanding of time, space and causality. They can now relate perceptions to one another, such as today to yesterday and tomorrow, cause to effect, an action to its justification, etc. They practice this mostly unconsciously at first but the process becomes increasingly conscious as they approach school maturity. As a result of this development children now use more advanced linguistic structures such as sub-clauses and conjunctions (because, if, although, while) and their sentences become more and more complex and demanding.

It is not language that drives this process, but rather thinking that precedes language and makes use of the manifold linguistic means to express the structures that are now understood. Thinking is the light that illumines the darkness of the wide, complex world and allows the thinker to become aware of him- or herself. An amazing dual process takes place: the individuality awakens the still dormant thinking and, in doing so, gains consciousness of itself.

The I awakens

It is a deeply incisive event in the life of young children when they begin to experience themselves as separate from the world and therefore cease to address themselves from the outside in the third person. Now for the first time children call themselves by the name that we each can only use for ourselves: "I."

Philosophically speaking this is the I/world dualism that is so familiar to us as adults and has been since puberty. We therefore tend to make the mistake of assuming that it is the same for young children. But for them this separation is totally new and constitutes a crisis that will fundamentally change the young child's self-image and relationship to others.

This crisis can manifest quite dramatically in the "terrible twos" when the child rigorously and with much emotion rejects what was happily accepted not that long ago. As adults we are well advised to see these tantrums as what they really are: the children do not want to hurt the people they love; they do not act out of malice. They take every opportunity to "rub" against resistance as this rubbing again and again affirms their independence and autonomy. They do not rejoice in the opposition but in the safety and the affirmation that "I am an I."

This experience of the conscious I becoming free signifies the real beginning of the earthly journey, and it is deeply meaningful that for all of us it is the time of our first memories. We cannot remember anything that happened before this point despite the fact that we achieved so much then: we learned to stand up, talk and think.

The phase before the I awakens clearly requires very particular educational support that even needs to be reflected in the outer environment. The time when children's learning is still entirely unconscious requires particular conditions that are not, or not sufficiently, provided in the kindergarten. A protected educational space is needed where young children can learn and practice the faculties they will need to develop before they can move on to kindergarten, when they have achieved what early childhood educators refer to as "kindergarten readiness."

5. The child's invisible helpers

The first two-and-a-half to three years in the life of a child are special, as self-awareness is still dormant and children are still devoted unconditionally to the surrounding impressions and influences. It is because of this lack of consciousness that children so wholly identify with the world and this is what enables them to learn with an intensity that will never be achieved again in later life. At no point in our later lives will we be able to learn at so many levels in such a short time as in those first three years.

It might sound like a paradox, but the still dormant self-awareness of children is the most essential foundation for mastering the three first and biggest tasks of child development: learning to walk, speak, and think. These are such enormous achievements that as adults today we would never be able to reproduce them consciously and of our own accord. Modern science is only beginning to unravel the mystery of earliest childhood.

How can young children manage these mammoth tasks while being so deeply unaware? There is reliable evidence that children do not begin to walk upright, speak, and think out of a biological necessity or due to a law of nature. They do these things because they are inspired by the example of adults. Yet, as adults we do not set out to teach these skills. We would not be able to teach them, since we are just as unaware of the foundations of skills we once acquired as the children are. We have no memory of how we integrated the skills of walking, speaking, and thinking into our physical bodies.

Rudolf Steiner's spiritual scientific findings (see for example *The Spiritual Guidance of the Individual and Humanity*) describe that the human being does not have the universal knowledge and wide-ranging skills needed for these early childhood achievements. The child receives them from the spiritual world, from higher beings whose wisdom and creative powers go far beyond what we as human beings could achieve. Human beings can partake in their powerful activities only in a condition of deep unconsciousness. Their influence abates as soon as our earthly consciousness awakens and we become self-reliant beings.

As adults we still experience this influence when we are exhausted from our day's work and in need of new enlivening impulses for our organism. We will only receive them if we enter a state of deep unconsciousness again; we go to sleep. When we sleep, the creative powers work on our organism, which is also the reason why babies and toddlers spend such a large part of the day sleeping.

C. Early Childhood Care and Education

The practice of early childhood care and education is informed by a range of experiences and principles that arise from the anthropological and methodological considerations described in the previous chapter. There are no universal rules, since Waldorf-oriented early childhood care programs differ depending on the legal requirements and economic conditions of a particular location, the situation of the families in the area, the qualifications of educators and care providers, and also the particular qualities of the children in attendance. We can therefore only provide guidelines that can be adapted to each particular situation.

There are, nevertheless, four fundamental principles that apply whatever the location or circumstances:

1. Early childhood educators need to establish a strong relationship with each child.
2. The children need to be able to move freely and play independently.
3. The environment must be suitable for young children.
4. The daily routine must be based on reliable rhythms and rituals.

1. Establishing the relationship — the foundation of early childhood care

Looking after very young children is a great responsibility. The nurturing and care of very young children, provided until recently in the family home, are often entrusted today to early childhood educators who take on the tasks of looking after the young children's basic needs and of fostering the development of motor skills and speech, as well as emotional and social competence.

As early childhood educators and caregivers we need to see to the children's physical needs in a way that is age-appropriate, but over and above that, we need to care for their soul life by establishing a warm and intense relationship with them. Very young children are different from kindergarten children: they need an attachment figure to whom they can turn whenever they feel the need for physical closeness. It is their only way of finding reassurance and safety. Infants live entirely in the present. They cannot conjure up the image of their parents and feel sure of their love when their parents are not there. They live fully in the here and now and have a constant need for reassurance.

Infants need to feel accepted by the new attachment figure in their lives in order to feel secure. When this sense of security is established, they devote themselves cheerfully to their "developmental tasks" and begin to explore the world and make contact with others. A reliable rhythm in the care situation, for example with feeding and diapering, helps the young child to bond with the new attachment figure and enter into a dialog with her. If conflict situations should arise, young children need to be able to withdraw to this haven of safety.

Early childhood educators must acquaint themselves with the laws of child development described earlier and be aware of the crucial difference in approach required for infants and toddlers compared to kindergarten children. The time leading up to nursery/kindergarten entry, at the age of about three to three-and-a-half years, is a special period when the relationship between caregiver and child is particularly intense. Educators and caregivers for children from birth to three years therefore need special training.

Preparing for the adjustment to a new situation

Preliminary note: Supporting children's adjustment to a new early childhood setting needs to be based on a thorough, well-conceived, age-appropriate approach. The model presented here has been applied successfully in the birth-to-three group of a Waldorf kindergarten in Berlin. It meets the requirements of the so-called Berlin Adjustment Model developed by Joachim Laewen of the INFANS Institute (Institute for Applied Socialization Research).

For one- to two-year-olds to spend a large part of the day in new surroundings, with many other children of the same age and unfamiliar adults, is an enormous challenge. But while this situation does not correspond to the developmental needs of infants and toddlers, it can still be managed in a way that safeguards the child's healthy development.

A gentle, step-by-step settling-in period is paramount. Each child is unique and we must read from the individual child when he or she is ready for the next step to keep the settling-in process as stress-free as possible. Once the caregiver is sure that the child feels safe and comfortable with her even when the child is in a vulnerable situation (due to pain of separation, conflict, fears, injuries), a secure bond can be said to have been established.

With this age group the educator needs to actively build up a relationship with the child. This is a lot easier if she is able to establish an empathic rapport with the parents, based on trust, understanding, and acceptance. Fears, insecurities, and ambivalent feelings can then be kept to a minimum.

Parents can take a first step by attending an information evening or open house before their child enters the program. An admissions interview follows that offers educators the chance to explain the child care program's philosophy. These meetings

THE CHILD FROM BIRTH TO THREE

offer both parties the opportunity to air their concerns and ideas and ask questions regarding the care situation. Educators and parents can get to know each other and come to mutually satisfactory agreements on issues that are important to them.

It has proved successful to ask returning parents to describe their first experiences with the child care center to new parents at parents' evenings. Caregivers can then explain the positive aspects but also the difficulties that can arise from the new experiences and relationships in the young child's life. The entire process can be enriching for children and parents at several levels if the adults involved maintain close contact and are prepared to share their concerns with each other. Children are at risk if they cannot cope with the new situation or if the parents' relationship to the caregiver becomes clouded by feelings of competition, fear or sadness.

Gentle separation from the parents

Once it has been established who will be the young child's primary caregiver in the child care center, she should meet with the parents to prepare a settling-in plan. The details of this plan will depend on the individual child's stage of development, the family situation, and the group of children. Although one will come to certain agreements in the course of this conversation, there needs to be a degree of flexibility since the next step of the settling-in process can only ever be taken when the individual child is ready for it. Young children sense the feeling of trust between their new attachment figure and their parents and it helps them to come in to the new situation.

The separation from the family home is rarely motivated by the children at this age, as they are still too intimately attached to their parents. It is essential that parents firmly decide that they really want the child care situation and the periods of separation from their children that it will necessarily involve. The firmer their resolution, the easier it will be for parents to entrust their child to the caregiver with a calm conscience.

It is important to emphasize this strength of determination, as parents often find themselves torn by ambivalent feelings: they feel the need for relief and more freedom on the one hand, while they are still almost "symbiotically" attached to their child on the other. Educators need to take the situation and all parental fears and doubts very seriously, while at the same time radiating professional confidence.

Parental fears affect the children right down into the physical organization. Establishing a bond of trust with the parents will help the educator to establish a secure attachment to the child.

The settling-in period

Like grandparents and other family friends, early childhood educators and caregivers can become secondary attachment figures to young children if they approach the situation with due sensitivity. An intimate relationship needs establishing; it does not develop by itself. Research on babies and infants (using MRI and cortisol testing) has shown that care situations carry the risk of causing insecurity and stress in very young children in the first two years of their life. The age when children first start day care and the number of hours a day they stay there are also important factors. Parents and educators must be aware of the fact that the time spent in the care situation can adversely affect infant development if it is not possible to establish a solid relationship between the child and the new attachment figure. Young children need roots, and these roots need time to grow in the new attachment.

As care providers we need to devote the greatest possible care to the settling-in period and to building up a strong relationship and secure bond with the young child. Child and caregiver need to become familiar with one another first. During this period one of the parents needs to be present. Only after a minimum of two weeks can a gradual separation be attempted. For very young children, it is easier to get used to a new attachment figure, new surroundings, other children, and the child care routine if a parent is present. Parents will also find it easier to develop trust in the child care staff if they have this direct experience of their child's new life.

We need to be highly perceptive as educators to distinguish between the children who start playing immediately and those who do not show signs of separation anxiety and do not seek contact with us although they are experiencing severe physical and emotional stress, as there is a heightened danger of lasting damage with this type of child (the "avoidant insecure" attachment pattern).

Educator and parents as partners

The term "parent-teacher partnership" is commonly used today and aptly characterizes the relationship we described above. A relationship informed by openness, respect, and empathy, where both sides communicate at eye-level, can only be mutually beneficial. The educator learns from the parents, who know the child and his or her special characteristics best, and the parents learn from the educator, who knows about child development and observes, with that knowledge in mind, the developmental steps taken by the individual child. Good communication between both parties is the best foundation for an appropriate care situation where the specific needs of each child are met. For children from single-parent families the caregiver represents an important extension to the relationship structure.

Home visits are helpful

Once children have settled into the child care setting and are able to stay without a parent, a home visit is recommended. For the children this is an important event since their new attachment figure enters their own world at home. It helps to take a colleague along who can chat with the parents while the child shows her caregiver where she plays, sleeps and eats.

The home visit enhances the building up of trust and offers educators the possibility of gaining a picture of the child's home environment, which will enable them to better understand when the child uses a single word to describe a much larger set of relationships. Older siblings and other family members also get to know the new attachment figure in the child's life, a circumstance that will further promote the settling-in process.

Bonding takes time

No matter at what point during the first three years the settling into the child care situation begins it will need considerable time, often several weeks. The little ones were, after all, never before separated from their parents, and there is nothing to reassure them that their parents will come back. Infants and toddlers have neither a rational understanding of the situation nor a sense of time. Very gradually and through constant repetition they learn that their parents will return. The stress involved in this process can only be reduced by a caregiver who has become another attachment figure and whom they have learned to trust.

The need for a "safe haven"

In the first two years of life children need a reliable primary caregiver who will change their diapers, put them to sleep, and be there in the morning when the parents leave. This attachment figure remains important in the third year and should not change. Not only does she instill a feeling of safety in the child, she also represents the essential counterpart for the child's awakening I or self-awareness. Children need somebody whom they deeply trust in order to be able to act out their tantrums and test the boundaries in the care situation.

Even in their third year, children who attend child care do not primarily come to a group of peers, but to their caregiver. With her, they

Helping the child to become competent

feel at home and safe due to the strong relationship that has been established. Out of this sense of security grows the child's ability to relate to other children, to enjoy or tolerate their behavior and to learn how others are different. This, in turn, enables the child to experience his or her individuality as separate from other individualities, especially in conflict situations.

Experiencing the relationship through physical care

Children under the age of three experience the world with their bodies as the part of their personality that has become autonomous. Soul and mind are not yet independent, but still intimately interwoven with the physical organization. By caring devotedly for this bodily being, we nurture, support and enhance the development of the whole person—body, soul and spirit.

To respect the dignity of such small children means first of all to give them the best possible care. We need to prepare the care situation and environment well so that we can give our full attention to the dialogue with the young child. We always let the child know what will happen next, by word or gesture, until the child's body language shows that he or she is ready to actively respond.

The Hungarian physician Emmi Pikler demonstrated convincingly in her orphanage what can be achieved with such simple means as the affectionate dialogue between caregiver and child in the daily care routine. She described examples from her practice that show how the children's joy in everyday situations, as well as their development and autonomy, are enhanced if we patiently wait for them to take action and then respond to them.

Eye contact, gestures, touch, and sounds make up this dialogue and create an atmosphere that is hard to describe but profoundly informs the encounter between the two individualities. The children experience affection, care, attention, and communication on many levels. Besides nourishing the soul, this stimulates the development of speech, social skills, self-awareness, body-awareness and motor skills. There is no better way for us to get to know and love the young individuality in its uniqueness than these short periods of time in the day when our full attention is directed at the child and vice versa. This quality time together must recur rhythmically and reliably so that the infant can anticipate it. Having been nurtured physically and emotionally in this way, the child will happily play or go to sleep.

Language from the beginning

The pedagogical use of language has been described in an earlier chapter but it should be underlined again that being surrounded by an ambient language is as vital for babies as breathing and nourishment. From the very beginning language is a nurturing element and without it, neither body, soul, nor spirit can grow in the right way.

There was a time in the past when it would not have been necessary to point this out, because parents used to speak to their babies long before the babies were able to articulate their first words and sentences. Parents today often do not speak to their children, thinking that communication is not yet possible. Recent research has confirmed, however, that the communicative skills of infants are widely underestimated. Even if they do not yet articulate syllables and words, they communicate through body language, gestures, movements, facial expressions, and sounds. If we pay attention to this multitude of messages, a lively dialogue can unfold. There are plenty of opportunities for this to happen in the care situation, but we need to take the time for it and we must not communicate with other people over the child's head.

When we communicate with infants we should not slip into baby talk. The fully developed language we use as adults is necessary for children and needs to surround them so that they can learn to speak. This does not mean that we can never playfully pick up the baby's babbling and gurgling sounds, but we must not stop at that. Even if conversations with babies seem like monologues at first, they are the grounds from which a real exchange can grow, if we learn to listen to the baby's non-verbal utterances and respond to them with spoken words. Babies love being perceived and being heard, and they listen intensely at the same time. They bathe in the cosmos of formed sounds, words, and sentences that we provide for them when we speak.

Once children begin to speak single words, we do best to answer them in normal language to enable them to expand their vocabulary and acquire new grammatical and syntactical structures. A young child who points at a car and says "vrrrm, vrrrm" does not expect us to do the same. It is much better if we confirm the observation with a sentence such as "Oh yes, there's a car." If it's the garbage truck we can call it that, perhaps adding a simple explanation.

Explanations should always relate to what is sense-perceptible and concrete to the children and not to a context they did not ask about. Children initially explore the world through perception, and that applies also to language. If, as educators, we use a rich vocabulary, songs, rhythmical verses, fun words and spontaneously made-up rhymes, we provide more "food" for the children's linguistic development than by supplying intellectual instructions.

2. Free movement and independent play

What is most essential and educational in play is that we put our rules and pedagogical efforts to one side and leave the children to their own powers. They will then try out, in their play, what effect this or that activity may have on the objects around them. They activate their own will. And by observing how things in the outside world respond to will-influence, children learn from life through play, in quite a different manner than they would do through the influence of a person or their pedagogical principles. It is therefore so very important that we introduce as little intellectual thinking as possible into the child's play.

—From Rudolf Steiner, "Human History in the Light of Spiritual Science"
Lecture of March 14, 1912, Berlin

These words are an appeal to us grown-ups to respect children's play as an act of self-education that is valuable in itself. There is no need for us to interfere with their spontaneous, vivid, active interaction with the outside world by introducing our own ideas into the process. If children are allowed to follow their own impulses when they play, they can awaken the dormant powers within them in a way that educational instructions cannot. The very first motor development is a creative, self-induced, active learning process that children use to educate themselves. They do not need to be instructed.

We will find it easier to resist interfering when we understand that the significance of play does not lie in serving some final purpose. It is an end in itself, an activity in which children can test and activate their own powers. It makes children happy to experience their own efficacy; it inspires them to more playing which again promotes their autonomy and self-confidence.

While we must refrain from interfering with children's free play, we can support them by creating the right conditions for a deeply fulfilling play experience:

- Children, especially infants, only play if they feel happy and safe.
- Children love an atmosphere permeated by creative activity. They are most easily inspired to activity if we carry out tasks around them that are practical, useful and that make sense to them.

- Very young children need to be able to take a rest during play time. They must have the possibility to withdraw from time to time and be close to the caregiver, where they feel at ease and can relax.

- For children to be able to deeply enter into play they need a daily structure and rhythm that provide them with the certainty: I can play safely here.

- We need to protect young children from sensory overload, which is not an easy task in a child care situation where there are always other children around. If children of different developmental stages are together, some individual children might be prevented from playing quietly, for example when some are so excited about their newly acquired walking skills that they are completely caught up in and excited by this new activity. At least in the warmer months, experience has shown that it is good to spend as much time as possible outside. If the outside play area is large enough, the various developmental stages can unfold without interfering with one another. Noise levels also tend to be less of a problem outside.

Even if we do not directly intervene in the children's play, our behavior around the children has a powerful effect, either beneficial or detrimental. We enhance the children's play if we handle tools and objects with care, concentrate on what we are doing, and address children in a natural and calm manner. On the other hand, talking that disrupts the children's devotion to pure activity and leads them to consciously distance themselves from their play by becoming self-conscious or reflective, is a hindrance. This includes intellectual and abstract explanations and instructions as well as constant praise or disapproval. Play time and free activities are the children's "work" and, like the work of adults, should not be interrupted.

Children often enjoy having time to themselves. If, however, they need the resonance of an adult to their creative "productions," it takes great sensitivity to know when to appropriately acknowledge what the child has achieved or created. When children feel perceived, they immediately feel reaffirmed in their actions.

By creating the right kind of environment and making inspiring materials available, the adult can further enhance the child's play. A number of suggestions are described below.

Free play in the child's first year

In the first year of life, a baby's free play is mostly focused on exploring the body and the immediate surroundings. One of the first great achievements is grasping things, followed a little later by learning to let go again.

We can enrich babies' play with their own hands and feet by giving them a piece of cloth or other objects as they grow older. A woven rattan ball is ideal for exploring because of the gaps between strands of material that allow for easy grasping and holding.

For children who grow up in a city and rarely have the opportunity to move freely on uneven ground in a garden or woods, we recommend building a ramp out of a flat box and a plank, to provide opportunities for discoveries and new experiences. Stools of various shapes and sizes have also proved successful.

First push-ups

Children love creating sounds. They eagerly take up all sorts of objects and bang them on a surface, listening carefully to the noise they produce. Ordinary objects such as saucepans, wooden spoons, dustpans, and brushes are very attractive and should be accessible to children as long as they are safe.

Toward the end of their first year, infants start taking things out of cupboards and putting them back again. For this they need materials such as pinecones, chestnuts, shells, and wooden balls, along with baskets, bowls, cups, bags, and boxes. Containers that fit into one another are particularly suitable. Wooden blocks are interesting because they can be placed in a long line and, in the second year, balanced on top of each other.

Baby's first doll should be quite simple, knotted from a piece of fabric to stimulate the child's imagination. It should not be too thin or too light, so that children have something to hold in their arms. It is best to use a square of fabric knitted from thick silk yarn, as that will hardly pill even if the children suck on it.

Very young children do not yet play with one another, but they like to pursue the same activities next to each other. This means that of each kind of plaything or toy there should be several available, because infants are not yet able to wait or share. At this age they are purely concerned with themselves and if they feel inspired by another child's playing, they should be able to play with the same kind of toys.

Younger children generally need bigger toys. They like feeling the impact of their own strength and they experience themselves in the resistance they encounter. It is best to use big wooden blocks and planks. As the children grow older, their fine motor skills also develop, and the toys can begin to be smaller.

A heap of sand outdoors supports the children's fine motor development because of the many opportunities it offers for touching and shaping. At the same time it allows for gross motor development and whole-body experiences, because the children can climb or roll on it or jump down from it.

Free play in the child's second year

Children extend their range of movements in the second year when they start climbing. Three-sided climbing frames are useful if there are no easy-to-climb trees in the garden.

Young children love carrying things from one place to another. Little sandbags can be used for this, or bags that are filled with spelt or with cherry or plum stones and covered in pretty fabric. They offer a variety of tactile experiences and enhance bodily perception. Children can put them on or next to their body in the hammock, let them slide down a ramp, or push their feet into the outer cover and go "skating." Children are never short of new ideas.

If the outside playground is not too uneven, we can supply "wobble boards" for the children to exercise their sense of balance. These are large wooden discs that are flat on top and rounded underneath so that they can tilt in all directions.

When the children have reached the age of about

Playing with and alongside one another

a year and a half they begin to play make-believe games. They feed sand to the rocking horse in the playground or pretend to "eat" the strawberries and chocolate they see on a poster, or they might put a doll into a shoe and pretend she is sailing away in a boat.

Ordinary objects like small saucepans, jugs, spoons, brushes, hobby-horses, pieces of fabric, ribbons, and all the things we recommended for the first year, when children empty and fill cupboards, are also very useful for pretend games. Dolls are particularly suitable for children to imitate everyday situations. For young children, dolls are best made of soft material with a rounded body that ends in a sleeping bag rather than legs. If children see how an adult draws or paints they become interested and want to draw too. They only need a surface and a few beeswax block crayons to draw "pictures" with a few strokes, corresponding to their stage of development.

Little buckets, spades, old cooking pots, and small wheelbarrows are wonderful outside toys. Balls of various sizes should be available so the children can practice giving and taking, rolling and catching, throwing and kicking. And water, of course, brings endless opportunities for joyful learning.

How far can I go?

Free play in the child's third year

In the third year children begin to imitate sequences of related activities. They will cook for and then feed their dolls, or put the shopping into a bag and carry it to the doll's house where they unpack it and begin to cook. They like dressing the doll in a sleeping bag, then taking her to bed and singing to her. For this "sequential play" it is good to have a doll's house and equipment needed to care for the dolls such as fabrics, blankets, little sleeping bags, beds, scales, and the items mentioned earlier.

Natural materials are most suitable, as they stimulate the children's imagination and offer many opportunities for the fantasy games that appear at the end of this year, when children begin to allocate ever-new meanings to things. At the end of the third year we occasionally see the first role-playing, when children begin to involve each other in their games.

Motor skills continue to develop. Most children can climb onto the swing or slide by themselves, which offers them

THE CHILD FROM BIRTH TO THREE

exciting body experiences. They like digging deep holes in the sand with spades, sometimes even in small groups, or they sweep leaves into a big pile. Playing with spinning tops or threading big beads are activities that promote fine motor skills.

3. The environment

The rooms and areas of the child care setting must be appropriate to the needs of very young children and all equipment must be chosen with early development in mind.

Room arrangement

In their first year, infants primarily develop their movement skills, and the rooms need to be equipped to accommodate this need. We need to consider that young children always need a bit more space than what they have already "conquered." Once they have learned to roll over to one side, they need a larger space than their crib during the times when they are awake. They also need a firm surface that gives them a feeling of their body position.

An area that offers enough space for rolling, while being secured by wooden play gates, will be safe and at the same time easy to supervise. The partitions are flexible and can be adjusted to accommodate the movement radius of one or several children. Up to the age of about two-and-a-half, children always need be able to see their caregiver or hear her voice.

A group of very young children will need more space than kindergarten children because they otherwise irritate each other, and conflicts will arise between the children who are not yet developmentally ready to practice social skills. Especially in the foyer or entrance hall, toddlers need plenty of space so they can take off or put on their coats in winter or in rainy weather. This is a valuable time for caregiver and child to work with care together, and it should be stress-free.

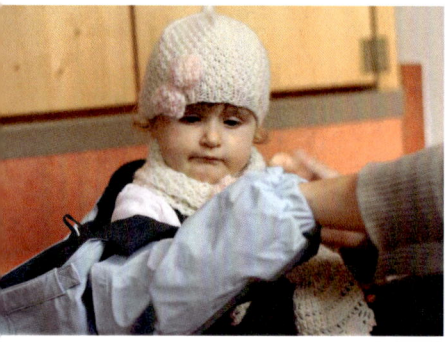

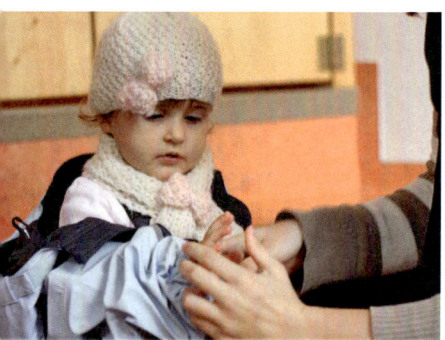

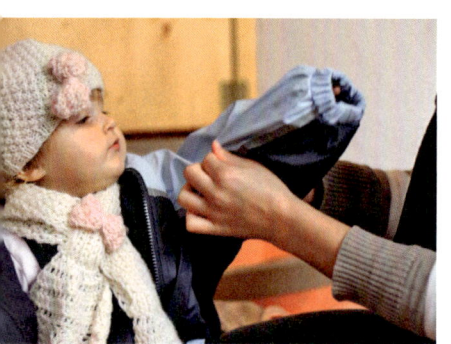

Where did the hand go?

The decoration of the child care room is an important consideration, as the children spend a fair amount of time there. It is here that the foundations are laid for the child's later aesthetic sensibility. For this reason, garish colors and busy patterns should be avoided. Natural materials help to create a warm atmosphere.

The diapering area

The rooms should be set up in a way that allows the children to observe the purposeful domestic or artistic activities of the adults. As we mentioned earlier, children educate themselves in perceiving and imitating adult role-models. If we separate off the diapering area from the remainder of the room using wooden gates, we can create a protected space where caregiver and child can be closely together while other children are still able to witness their presence and the care-giving activity. This will leave a deep impression and will find its reflection in their play with dolls later on.

The diapering surface must offer enough space for the child to move around and it must be at a height that allows the caregiver to be at eye level with the child. It is best if a ladder leads up to it, so that the children can climb up on their own as soon as they feel confident to do so.

Climbing up to the changing table

This enhances their motor skills, promotes autonomy, and is easier on the caregiver's back. Everything needed for diapering must of course be in easy reach.

Mealtimes

Eating is a cultural skill that children acquire in several stages. We start by feeding the baby on our lap, allowing him or her to touch our arm but not the spoon or the food. We help the children with drinking while they hold the cup.

The second stage begins when the child pick up the glass, drinks from it and hands it back to us. Children can now sit in an eating bench or highchair to eat. Highchairs have the disadvantage of restricting the children's movement and preventing them from being able to get up or down by themselves. If we use an eating bench, the children have to learn not to play with their food or cutlery, not to get up during meals, and to finish one piece of food before starting on the next. It helps if we sit opposite the child and gently support the learning process. Since this process requires an atmosphere of peacefulness and concentration, we can protect the eating area by separating it off with wooden gates.

THE CHILD FROM BIRTH TO THREE

Offering and accepting

When the children are between sixteen and eighteen months old, they can usually sit safely around a table together. For this they need chairs that allow them to sit upright and put their hands on the table, their arms forming a right angle at the elbow, while their feet are placed firmly on the ground to give stability and ensure a certain stillness.

Eating in the group is more tiring than in a one-on-one situation. It is best to start with two to four children at one table and later extend the group by adding more tables.

If we want the children to benefit from the adult's example, we need to sit at the table with them, making sure we sit as comfortably as possible and with good posture. Kindergarten tables are usually high enough and offer the advantage that the children can observe the routine activities adults carry out there when it is not mealtime. The children's chairs that go with the tables are slightly higher with adjustable footrests. Since the footrests need to be set to the height of the individual child, each chair needs to be labeled. We recommend using the same image that marks the child's coat rack. Very young children love having their own places within the group. They are still developing self-awareness and are therefore allowed to be "selfish." This individual touch is particularly important during the phase when they resolutely insist on things being "mine." It also helps if they bring their own dolls to the child care setting.

Reaching for independence

Whatever the details of our arrangements, we must keep in mind that mealtimes are not just there for eating, but are an important part of social life. Stress-free and enjoyable mealtimes will enhance the well-being and digestion of all involved.

The sleeping area

Sleeping without their parents and in new surroundings is a considerable challenge for very young children. The settling-in process must have progressed well before this can happen and the children must feel safe and confident with their new attachment figures, as they will otherwise not be able to relax and let go. Infants fall asleep more easily in a confined space such as a bed with a canopy. A sleeping bag will convey in an understandable way the idea that it is time for the gross motor system to have a rest.

Experiencing nature

Experiencing nature should be part of the daily routine and it is best to find a place close to the building where one can take the children regularly. The

Want one?

diverse stimulation offered by nature nurtures the children's foundational senses (touch, movement, balance and life) and general health. Children need air and light, and moving and running around outside exercises their breathing and circulation. Babies also depend on sunlight for building up strong and healthy bones.

4. Rhythm and rituals

Very young children in a child care situation rely to an even greater extent than kindergarten children on transparent processes and clear daily rhythms for safety and orientation. They find it difficult to cope with unforeseen events; regularity and rhythm help them to experience their growing competence, as they choose to join in or—during their terrible twos—offer energetic resistance.

Much of what we ask of kindergarten children cannot be expected of children under the age of three: they are not yet able to accommodate to the needs of the group, sit still, or concentrate on an ongoing process for a long period of time. The daily rhythm in the child care setting depends on the children's rhythm of sleep, and we can only begin to establish a group rhythm with children who sleep only once a day, from the age of about one and a half. With the younger ones we need to observe their individual sleeping and eating rhythms and give them plenty of time for playful exploration.

Small daily rituals that are familiar and enjoyable also offer additional support for the small child to feel secure and protected. Apart from the high standard of daily care that we offer the children, we can provide regular rituals that offer more than what is strictly necessary. Little children benefit immensely from very simple rituals, and if we are patient their positive effects on the children will reveal themselves. We can create moments of wonder, quiet listening and intimacy if we sing a pentatonic lullaby or gently play on a harp when the children have settled down to sleep. Such tones convey to the child that their trusted caregiver is still close by.

A little ritual

D. Conditions for Infant and Toddler Child Care

A number of conditions need to be in place for the pedagogical foundations and objectives described in Sections A and B to be put into practice as outlined in Section C. The conditions concern all aspects of the child care center, including legal bodies who carry responsibility for it, the educators and caregivers, and also the rooms and equipment. A number of basic guidelines will be given in this section.

1. The impulse behind Waldorf early childhood education

Society has changed in a way that makes it increasingly necessary for parents to seek professional day care for their very young children. Waldorf kindergartens can not ignore this societal trend and have begun to respond to its demands by starting child care programs for children under the age of three.

At the same time, scientific research into early childhood and brain development in recent years has revealed how immensely important early experiences are for an individual's entire later biography. These findings underline the fact that we cannot overestimate the responsibility implied in founding and running such a center for children under three. Everybody involved in such a venture, whether initiators, administrators or educators, must be fully aware of the responsibility they take upon themselves with regard to the children and their parents.

As described earlier, this responsibility includes aspects such as the early childhood educators' inner attitude and way of thinking, since they work in a formative way on the children's physical development and influence their future health, strength, resilience, and creativity. How well children will be able to think, communicate, and act in later life depends to a large extent on what they experience in their immediate surroundings at a very early age, not intellectually but in terms of hands-on, sensory experiences which will allow them to develop their motor skills, and in terms of the attachments they form with their caregivers. What emerges later as intellectual acuity, practical competence, social skills, and self-knowledge is founded on activities and experiences in early childhood that do not resemble their outcome.

These transformative processes (metamorphoses) will allow these early developments, which are always tied to the child's physicality, to ripen into emotional, mental and spiritual competencies. It is the central task of all early childhood care settings based on Waldorf education to foster and enhance this development in their daily practice, however different their unique outer conditions or circumstances might be.

Bonding and attachment

Research and actual practice have confirmed that it is possible, in some cases even helpful, for very young children to have a reliable secondary attachment figure in addition to the primary attachment to their parents, when the necessary requirements are met and a gentle settling-in process can take place. In this process it is important that the caregiver does not try to take on the mother's role. It is her task to build up a regular, warm, personal contact with the child at a professional level by providing, in the care situation, the supportive atmosphere and loving attention that children need for their development. If this is successful, the young child will be able to accept the educator as a secondary attachment figure in addition to their parents as primary caregivers, in the same way as they would accept relatives who are regularly around them and who have a good and harmonious relationship with the parents.

It is therefore important for the educator to maintain a good relationship with the parents. Considerable competence is needed for this, since it involves including the parents in all processes and supporting them if they struggle to come to terms with the early separation from their little ones.

Research and discovery with water

2. Standards of care for children under the age of three

Legal requirements for infant and toddler child care vary by state but usually include include the following:

- Sufficient space for each child
- Professional qualification of caregivers and continuing education requirements
- A specified educator-child ratio

The following additional guidelines apply to Waldorf child care settings:

- The educator-child ratio must allow for each child to receive the care and attention he or she needs.
- This applies particularly when slowly-developing children need to be settled in (which can happen more easily in child care than in kindergartens).
- There must be enough space for playing and moving around.
- There must be ample opportunity for sensory experiences and nature experiences.
- Special (age-appropriate and safe) toys and play structures need to be purchased, which involves considerable initial expense, and suitable materials need to be chosen carefully.
- Fostering child development and preventive measures are further important considerations. Collaboration with school doctors, therapists, curative teachers, and specialists is recommended.

3. Basic and advanced training

Training of Waldorf early childhood educators in general
Usually government regulations require educators working with young children to complete basic child care training. Special training opportunities for qualification as a Waldorf early childhood educator are available.

Specialist training for educators of children under the age of three
Fully trained Waldorf kindergarten teachers and state-trained educators with no additional Waldorf training need special qualifications for working with under-three-year-olds. The Worldwide Initiative of Early Childhood Care (WIEC) has developed guidelines for the training of caregivers.

Inner work and mental health
As part of their continuing education, early childhood educators and caregivers continue to deepen their specialist knowledge of all aspects of early childhood including motor development, speech development, mental and social development, etc. They must also be willing to continuously reflect on their work. Not only do they have to be fully aware of the effects of their actions at all times, but they must recognize and acknowledge their own strengths and weaknesses, since it is this self-knowledge that will provide the inner freedom upon which an empathic relationship with the young children and their parents can be built. Much depends on the educator's self-image, her willingness to work on herself and her further development, her ability to perceive in an unprejudiced way, and her striving for sensitivity in her work with young children. As an important step on the way to achieve these aims, Waldorf educators acquire and practice artistic capacities. It is this artistic sensibility that will allow them to become representatives of the "art of education" that distinguishes true Waldorf education.

Mental health is of the utmost importance, and educators might have to undergo a process of coming to terms with their own childhood (through counseling or biography work) to make sure that children will not be burdened with experiences of transference or counter-transference. The adults' daily endeavor to find the healthy middle, the right balance between firmness and flexibility, between inwardness and openness, is of the highest educational value. Working with very young children requires strict consistency on the one hand, as similar actions are repeated day after day; on the other hand, it needs a high degree of flexibility in any new situation that arises. In other words, educators have to be masters of the situation at all times.

Educators must be role-models who continue to develop so that they can inspire the developing child to imitation. Gaining self-knowledge and unfolding one's inner potential are also part of the anthroposophical inner development that Rudolf Steiner recommended and that forms the foundation of Waldorf education.

The required development of awareness in thinking, feeling, and doing will constitute the source from which the educator gains energy and resilience for the daily work with the children and their parents, and from which she or he receives the joy in performing educational tasks that is essential in order to work in a salutogenic way with young children.

4. Rooms, furnishings and equipment

Child care centers for children under the age of three need to provide a protective space, socially as well as emotionally, where the all-important first developmental phase, in which the foundations are laid for later life, can unfold undisturbed. In this phase, this is, strictly speaking, foremost the task of parents and family. If this task is entrusted to other caregivers for some of the child's day, they must apply the highest standards of care in the best possible surroundings. Young children need the following:

- A room where they can sleep undisturbed
- A diapering area (see below)
- A play area that is adaptable to the various developmental stages
- A group space that is large enough so that smaller areas can be partitioned off for the various developmental stages, for example a crawling area for babies who want to explore but are not walking yet
- Enough play items of the same kind, because children of this age are not yet able to share or to consider the needs of others
- Suitable materials, indoors as well as outdoors, that foster the child's foundational senses (touch, life, movement, balance)
- Areas and equipment that are safe enough to allow children to move freely without needing constant intervention or restriction from the caregivers

THE CHILD FROM BIRTH TO THREE

When we furnish the rooms we need to make sure that we create a pleasing, nurturing space in which we cater to the two most important needs young children have (next to sleeping): playing, moving, and exploring on the one hand, and being cared for and nurtured on the other.

Play and movement

Children under the age of three need a protected space where they can move and explore according to their development. Once they can walk they need structures to climb onto or to walk in and out of.

At this early age, children play with the whole body and they need challenges that correspond to this stage. Toys and materials that foster fine motor skills are only appropriate in the third year when the thinking begins to develop. Multi-colored building blocks will then become a favorite, as the children find infinite ways of sorting them and build towers as high as they are. Play now becomes restricted to one place and tends to happen in a particular part of the room.

Having ample opportunity for free play and movement leads to children who are autonomous in their actions, which is the ideal basis for their self-education and for developing a wide range of competencies. It is here that the foundations are laid for the future ability to take appropriate action in life and to develop the original trust from which a healthy self-confidence can grow.

The diapering area

Even physical care and diapering can take place in a way that enhances the child's development. In devoting enough time, attention, and respect to the evolving individuality, the caregiver fosters the child's communication skills that form the ground from which social skills can later arise. Although legal regulations sometimes

stipulate that the diapering area should be in a separate room for reasons of hygiene, in Waldorf child care settings they are ideally in the main play room, but partitioned off with play gates. In this way the caregiver can devote her full attention to the child she cares for, while still having an awareness of the other children who, in turn, unconsciously absorb the devotion and respect of her caregiving and will apply it in dealing with each other.

Eating and sleeping

The requirements for eating and sleeping have been described in Section C. It is essential that we create the right conditions so that children can enjoy their meals together in a relaxed atmosphere. This is much more important than the actual taking in of food. If mealtimes become stressful, it is a sure sign that something in the set-up needs changing.

Light

As with growing plants, appropriate light is also essential for young children. The room should be adequately and pleasantly lit and windows be arranged in a way that guarantees optimal light conditions.

Materials

Materials used should engage all the senses and lead children to experience the richness and diversity of the world around them. At this age the main purpose of such materials is to awaken the children's joy in exploring as they make the world their home.

For children, concepts arise gradually through tactile experiences. Once the children begin to become aware of each other, we need to offer more than one of the same materials, because the children are fully focused on what they are playing with at the moment and have no interest in anything else, yet they are not able to share or be taught to share. Young children tend to need bigger toys to enhance motor development. Moving heavy wooden blocks around gives them a sense of the impact they can have on their surroundings. The development of fine motor skills follows that of gross motor skills.

The outdoor environment

The outside play area must offer opportunity for sensory experiences, for example a small sand hill for climbing up, some steps and uneven terrain so that the senses

THE CHILD FROM BIRTH TO THREE

Learning through imitation and sensory experiences

of balance and movement are engaged. It is important to find the golden mean between avoiding the risk of injury (as with sharp edges, pointed fences, holes, etc.) and offering sufficient scope for the senses to develop through encounters with the outside world. The caregivers' sense of safety or anxiety and the attitude of parents are critical aspects. Open conversations with parents on the question of how much space children need can help to relax the situation.

In the outside play area we also use natural materials, as they stimulate the children's sense of touch and enhance their ability to discriminate between sensory experiences.

5. Legal and financial aspects

Waldorf education usually relies on private funding and support. The initiative for founding Waldorf kindergartens and birth-to-three programs often starts with the parents. Sometimes legal steps need to be taken so that an independent school or not-for-profit organization can be founded or its continued existence safeguarded. Waldorf institutions therefore support independence in education from early childhood up to higher education, all over the world.

Depending on the legislation and regulations in their country or region, some independent institutions have access to state funding, although this does not usually cover all their material and personnel costs, which means that parents have to pay tuition fees.

The name "Waldorf" is internationally protected. More information on this can be obtained from the Waldorf early childhood associations in various countries or from the International Association of Steiner Waldorf Early Childhood Education (IASWECE). The national associations and their specialist consultants make sure that each institution meets the criteria of Waldorf education.

Any initiatives interested in establishing a Waldorf birth-to-three or child care program should join the Waldorf early childhood association in their country, where they will receive help and advice.

6. Quality assurance and collegial work

Waldorf child care centers and institutions must meet quality assurance criteria such as the following:

- An educational vision statement that is regularly updated
- Binding regulations concerning the responsibilities of group leaders, interns etc.
- Regular work documentation (the extent needs to be established)
- Close cooperation of parents and educators
- Weekly pedagogical meetings that do not only deal with organizational issues but serve as ongoing pedagogical training
- Cooperation with educational specialists in the area on questions of
- quality development and professional practice
- Cooperation with pediatricians and therapists
- Ongoing continuing education for educators (such as taking part in regional, national and international birth-to-three conferences)
- Ongoing revision and, if necessary, adaptation of educational concepts to meet the demands posed by a rapidly changing society, new family and parent-child constellations, attitudes about children and parenting that have clearly changed, growing health concerns, and many other phenomena of our times.

Working in a team

High quality child care can only be provided if all members of staff work together harmoniously. Time for conversations, clear work structures, and good documentation and evaluation of the work are essential. The shared interest in the institution's educational concept, especially in the development of the children and their families, is particularly important. Regular meetings offer the opportunity to discuss children and topics such as early childhood development, anthroposophy, and parental participation.

Individual and shared reflection is also an important aspect of collegiality. Regular reflection on our habits and questioning our work will enhance our professional practice. Peer review or "intervision" gives individual educators the chance to see themselves through the eyes of a colleague. Making video recordings of certain aspects of the child care situation such as diapering (following mutual consent) is a useful tool in the evaluation of the entire child care team. Such recordings make us aware of elements in our work that we would not usually notice.

7. Working with parents

Children need their parents or other attachment figures for healthy development, especially when they are very young. Current lifestyles and growing parental individuation mean that growing numbers of children will be cared for by someone other than their mother before they reach their third birthday. The parents nonetheless remain the children's primary attachment figures, even if the children spend the greater part of the day in a child care setting.

In most countries there are clear legal regulations that govern the relationship between parents and such institutions. Over and above that, it is important for us as educators to bring the same attention and respect that we have for the children to the parents. Especially where very young children are concerned, trusting, open cooperation with parents is essential. We can inspire attitudes and habits that bring healthy rhythms to the children's lives and allow us to develop a professional, non-subjective attachment to them.

Parents and educators as partners

Independent educational institutions expect a strong commitment from parents and attachment figures that is consonant with pedagogical requirements, especially if the children are very young. Parental participation and mutual support between educators and parents are therefore of the greatest importance. We need to bear in mind, however, that parents who have their children in child care are working and the time they can spend with their children is therefore limited. This means that we have to make sure that their involvement in the child care setting is also nurturing and enriching for them and does not add to their burden.

The child's settling-in period is a good time to establish a positive relationship with the parents, as during this time, which may take up to three weeks, they get to know the routine. A warm welcome in the morning when the children are dropped off, time for a cup of tea together at pick-up time and, not least, the parents' evenings enhance parental participation.

Parental participation refers to the active involvement of parents as partners in the education of their children. Parents want to be perceived and taken seriously. If we understand our work as educational in the widest sense, activities such as festival preparation, redecorating the rooms, gardening work, and the offering of structural, organizational and financial support take on an entirely new meaning. Parents can play their part in this overall process by bringing in their own skills and professional competence where needed. Educators need to be confident and self-assured to be comfortable with this degree of openness.

8. Working with physicians, therapists and early childhood development specialists

Working together with physicians, therapists, and early childhood development specialists is part of the original concept of Waldorf education. As described in Section A, this concept

sees child development salutogenically, as an indivisible interplay of physical, emotional and spiritual processes and the social conditions in the environment. Close collaboration of physicians, educators, and therapists is therefore essential for healthy child development.

For parents whose children are in child care, organizing a support network that covers all their children's needs is often too much. The more closely early childhood educators work with physicians and therapists, the more relieved and supported families can feel. The fact that the various experts trust and have confidence in each other saves parents a lot of time and ensures that children are nurtured in the right way. Because parents need to authorize the release of confidential information, they become aware of the network of support that is attached to the provision of child care.

9. Working with kindergarten and school

For some time now, educational policies in many countries have focused on making the transition from kindergarten to school, from home to kindergarten, and from elementary to higher education, smoother and more transparent. Special models and curriculum guidelines have been developed and tested that cover education from birth to age ten or beyond. Scientific research also focuses on the issue of transitions. The transition from early childhood care to kindergarten forms part of these considerations.

From its very beginnings, Waldorf education has regarded child development as a biographical process that begins at birth and leads up to adulthood. We therefore welcome the fact that the traditional boundaries between kindergarten and elementary school and between elementary and high school are increasingly called into question and that efforts are being made to eliminate them. For these efforts to be successful, something needs to be in place that Waldorf education has not yet achieved: educators and teachers of all age groups need to collaborate. Early childhood educators and school teachers especially need to work together closely. We hear voices from many sides today demanding that we begin to take seriously our own principle that education begins with the child: the places where education happens need to be adapted to the children and not the other way round.

Cooperation between Waldorf child care settings and kindergartens in the neighborhood is a valuable first step that can lead to constructive contacts between Waldorf kindergartens and the schools in the area (not only Waldorf schools). Collaboration with the admissions departments and staff of Waldorf schools also needs to be developed.

10. Social integration

The recommendation to cooperate with similar educational institutions also extends to child care centers. This kind of integration into the social context is best achieved via a nearby kindergarten, school or family education center. Waldorf child care programs can offer parent education programs together with other centers in the area (kindergartens or parent-and-child groups) and in this way contribute to a better understanding of aspects of child development or of the minor or major concerns and problems that might arise in families.

Occasional meetings between similar educational institutions in the area can also be constructive, as the sharing of experiences and expertise promotes mutual understanding and can also be useful for pursuing common political or economic interests.

11. Starting a birth-to-three program within an existing institution

Many birth-to-three programs are founded as part of existing kindergartens and form a separate unit within the kindergarten organism. It is often one of the kindergarten teachers who makes it her or his special task and gives support to the initiative. If this endeavor is to be successful, it needs the support of the entire faculty of educators, board, and parents. The rationale for the founding of a birth-to-three child care program must be clearly described and carried by everyone involved, so that there is a solid foundation on which all further actions can build.

Difficulties are inevitable if the impulse to start a new program comes from the school's board or administration alone and is not supported by the teachers or educators. If they are excluded, they tend to see the endeavor as a purely financial enterprise intent on securing sufficient "numbers" for the kindergarten in the long term. A new initiative can only be successful if it has the support of all parties involved, if thorough discussions take place and agreements are achieved among the various interest groups.

Structural changes

The parties involved then have to focus on the consequences arising from their agreed intention to found a birth-to-three or child care program; one of these consequences is that the educators need to complete the necessary specialized training that will give them the professional qualification for the new task. This has financial implications that need to be considered. New buildings or extensions to existing buildings might be necessary that cannot be planned without the involvement of early childhood educators, since decisions regarding room design must be informed by important aesthetic and practical considerations for early childhood education.

The necessary changes will also affect the institution's overall organization and personnel structure. In order to offer families with several children a unified care situation, the opening times of child care and kindergarten need to be coordinated. The needs of parents must also be considered when opening times are established, to make sure that their family and working life can run as smoothly as possible. Having said this, the special quality of the parent-child relationship still needs to retain absolute priority.

Starting a birth-to-three program has other implications that might well be overlooked at first: when calculating the kindergarten's admission capacity for future years, it is important to bear in mind that the places available must be in a particular proportion to the number of infant and toddler places. This proportion arises from the time children spend in the birth-to-three program: children who are offered places in birth-to-three classes at the age of six months will enter nursery/kindergarten two-and-a-half years later, while children who start when they are one or two years old will need their nursery/kindergarten places much sooner. Apart from that, there have to be sufficient places for those children who enter the nursery/kindergarten at the age of three without having first attended the birth-to-three program.

Our work in the birth-to-three child care setting is, as was mentioned earlier, strongly influenced by the intensity of the relationship we are able to establish with the children and their families. Continuity is the highest priority in child care. It means reliability for the child and the parents, and it needs to be a guiding factor in personnel planning. In practice, this means that sickness coverage, for instance, must be well-planned, since one cannot simply have kindergarten teachers substitute for birth-to-three caregivers.

Collaboration among child care providers, kindergarten teachers and parents

For a successful care environment, it is essential that everybody involved, including the parents, have a clear picture of their own tasks and those of others. The kindergarten teachers should be aware, for instance, that their child care colleagues are under additional stress during settling-in times and that they might need relief in areas such as administration, event organization, festivals and fairs. The same applies to parents of infants and toddlers. Due to the very young age of their children, they cannot take on as many duties as kindergarten parents.

Shared meetings and study groups are essential if one wants to gain good mutual understanding of the tasks involved in kindergarten and child care. Such meetings allow for the fruitful sharing of pedagogical experiences and offer the opportunity to discuss the transition of children who are about to move up to kindergarten.

After the intensive support parents received from the birth-to-three program, caregivers and kindergarten teachers now have the joint task of preparing the parents, through conversations and advice, for the transition to nursery/kindergarten. If this does not happen, parents might feel left alone and look for another kindergarten. The seamless education from birth to eighteen that Waldorf education advocates is put to the test for the first time at this threshold between birth-to-three and kindergarten. The concept will only be convincing and successful if parents feel that their children are well supported by the caregivers and kindergarten teachers when they take this step from the familiar to the new situation. By actively working with each other and with the parents, the educators will be able to prevent a disruption in the child's educational biography. Smooth transitions are an essential aspect of an education that is based on child development.

12. Independent Learning and Relationship Learning

Basic phenomena of child development as an orientation for educational and therapeutic practice

At birth each child brings two primal experiences with it: connectedness and the ability to grow beyond one's self, thus two needs that manifest themselves as the will to relate and the will to create. In everyone this lives as a permanent longing, as homesickness and wanderlust. We have to create a framework in which what we wish for and need can happen. We need a culture where potential can unfold. We must invite people, encourage them, inspire them. Relationships are the most important thing today.
—Gerald Hüther[1]

As more toddlers and infants are cared for outside the family home, there is a growing need to understand what really happens during pregnancy, birth and early childhood. What used to take place in the private sphere of the domestic environment is becoming the responsibility of interdisciplinary cooperation between different professions as a network around the family, indeed as a social task in general.

As early as 1907, Rudolf Steiner emphasized the importance of the first three years of life for future health and biographical development. Early childhood experiences also played an important role in psychoanalysis, which was emerging at that time too. The fundamental influence of this phase of life has now become generally acknowledged in the fields of neurology and psychology.[2] At the same time, however, early childhood is now threatened by numerous social burdens and dangers, such as the steadily increasing Cesarean delivery rate and its psychosocial late effects compared to vaginal birth, the continuing lack of equal opportunities for children from socially disadvantaged families, and the growing phenomenon of children who have mentally ill parents. This is why specialists in education and medicine are increasingly working together with parents to develop appropriate institutional concepts for the care, upbringing, and health of children under the age of three.

Which basic phenomena can be assumed?

How do we arrive at fundamental insights as a basis for our specific professional actions? How can professional caregivers identify children's needs and support their healthy development? How can educators and health practitioners provide parents with comprehensible, meaningful, and practical orientation that will promote the development of young children in the family, while taking into account a wide range of cultural and religious backgrounds? How can we avoid making false claims and

EDUCATIONAL FOUNDATIONS AND OBJECTIVES

instead derive comprehensible knowledge from observable phenomena in which we can all participate as human beings?

First we must gain a basic understanding of what happens in anthropological terms during early childhood. First, we must know our guiding image of the human being, the basic assumptions from which we start. Is the child a physical product of his parents or surrounding conditions (epigenetics)? Is the ego a construct of the brain? A Christian or Islamic conception of the human being, with its consequences? And what extension does such a basic understanding gain by the assumption of a "persona" (a spirit), as in ancient Greece, which meets a kind of "model body" and forms the concrete hereditary material into a unique human individuality (Diagram 1)? These questions are fundamental to the attitude and intention of child-care professionals. They each lead to different answers regarding essential questions of the healthy development of the child as an individual personality and her later self-determination and ability to form relationships.

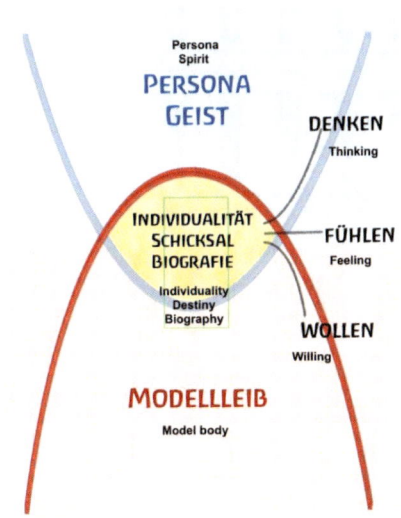

In the quotation that opens this article, Gerald Hüther concisely describes two universal experiences of infants and toddlers: A long-lasting dependence on other people, the foundation of human connectedness; and the will to "grow beyond one's self," to constantly grasp and discover new things. These opposing, basic needs are an expression of the child's will to relate on one pole and the will to create on the other pole. Today we know that this double potential has a lot to do with later overall health and the healthy development of learning and cognitive skills.

Diagram 1

Bonding through dialogical interaction in being together

The infant and small child are completely at the mercy of the environment, depending for all their needs on the care and protection of an adult. The previously lived primal experience of a united existence in pregnancy is gone; at birth, the first experience of boundaries and separation occurs. In the approximately 30,000 smile dialogues that parents normally offer their children in the first six months of life,[3] trust in a new unity between child and a reliable caregiver can be created. The child gradually learns the qualities of connectedness and security in the moments of being cared for by mother or father. The boundless basic trust initially shown to the

Diagram 2

world is confirmed. The child perceives the adult through the adult's actions, language, inner attitude, outlook, and so forth, then learns step-by-step to participate, eventually to become independent, self-sufficient, and responsible.

Encouraged by such positive experiences, the growing child in time becomes secure in his or her ability to interact with other people and circumstances. If positive experiences are lacking at this early stage, then dialogic encounters in the social sphere can become more difficult later in life. The moments of necessary togetherness during care in infancy are therefore decisive for the child's later ability to relate to other people. Adults who can be present in their moments of being together with children, especially when caring for them, taking their time and accompanying their actions with language, are more perceptible for their children and create trust in the environment through dialogue. In being together, a kind of sheath forms, and the bond between child and caregiver grows. This is also the case when we adults accompany children through diverse stages of their development and through repeated experiences of separation. The fact that people are reliable, that everything happens at the right time, that life has a rhythm, which is shaped by the adults – only this makes it possible to form a bond as an essential step in the development of the child's own personality. From the protective sheath formed by positive interactions grows security, love, and warmth, as fulfilled basic needs of the soul (Diagram 2).

This is expressed by caregivers through touch, sensory perception, resonance, nonverbal and verbal communication, and the joy of being together. The young child gains self-perception through being perceived. "I see and am seen, therefore I am," is how pediatrician and psychiatrist Donald Winnicott describes this process of becoming a self.[4] The strong emotional bond that develops between mother and child in the first months of life is therefore called "attachment" by British psychologist John Bowlby and is laer further differentiated by his colleague Mary Ainsworth. She recognizes different attachment patterns depending on the offers made by the attachment person.[5] The capacity for relationship and attachment develops from the offers of being together and is dependent on characteristics of communication between an attachment person and the child.

Independent earning through creative exploration

From birth, the child shows amazing abilities that cannot be taught or controlled from the outside and with which it finally achieves mastery in the world: his sucking reflex, his limb movements, the increasing focus of his gaze in his perception of the environment, and so on. His impulses and movements come entirely from within, according to laws that lie within him alone. Rudolf Steiner uses the term "will" for this early childhood activity and observes: ". . . adults have no possibilities to intervene in the will of the child. The child does what he wants! And he does so in a highly differentiated, active and extremely orderly manner."6

While self and world were still directly connected at birth, in the first year of life the child gradually comes to perceive that his mother's breast is a part of the world outside him. Likewise his own hand, which after much practice he can guide up to his mouth by himself. This continues with becoming upright and acquiring a differentiated capacity for movement in general. We see the developmental steps of the child from the arbitrary movements of the beginning of life to ever greater control of his own body, inspired by his conquest of the surrounding world, through continuous activity and infinite repetitions and variations.

This experience of the child's own movement is the basis for the child to discover his "own inner mover," his own creative power This enables to child to avoid remaining alien and separate from the world, to gradually take hold of the world in his own individual way. Experiences of separation on the other hand are necessary as steps towards human freedom. To later bring about the overcoming of separation, thanks to one's own activity and one's own drive, becomes the primordial experience of will activity, self-regulation, and control of one's own personality.

At birth, the child's physicality comes into gravity, but his organs only develop their forms and structures with increasing activity.7 In this process of individualization, uprightness is achieved and gravity is overcome in favor of light and lightness in life. The child can recognize more and more of his environment. However, he takes the individual time he needs to measure and shape the space around him, acquiring his own orientation in the relationship of time and space. Emmi Pikler formulated her guiding principle empirically, entirely from her observation of the child: "Give me time to do it myself!" In this way children learn about learning, a gesture they keep for the rest of their lives. Being on one's own in this process of discovery is a quality of learning. It shapes the powers of independence, self-determination, self-assessment, and boundaries of the future adult individuality. The way in which the child makes the foreign environment his own is the earliest experience of self-development. Perceived information must be recorded and processed. From my failures, I gradually learn to estimate how much force I need, for example, to pick up an object. This regulates my undertaking/performance in relation to the implementation. Movement and play are thus continuous training and correction of my own corporeality, the training and equipping of my organs and limbs.

When we observe children when they discover their hands and play with them, when they later try to stand and walk, or still later sort things or build something, we are so impressed by the concentration with which they carry out these activities on their own – if we do not disturb them. In movement and play, the child follows his own development through discovery and gradual conquest of the world. He explores the laws of how things are connected, follows movements and their starting point, becomes aware of objects, and so forth. This exploration fulfills the child's basic need for freedom, autonomy and creativity. He must be able to rest concentrated in himself in order to discover and grasp the world (Diagram 3).

Every child, indeed every human being, has this basic need to discover and organize things independently. If it is possible in this way to bring the doer and what is being done into alignment, then I perceive myself within it, and I feel: I am.

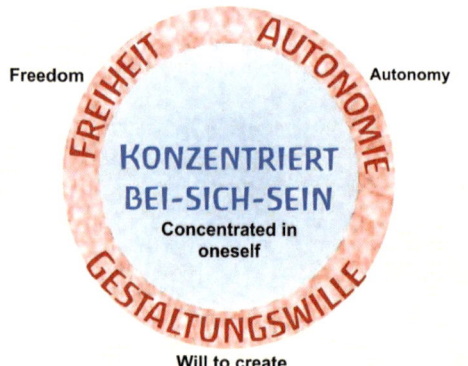

Diagram 3

In children, this sense of self initially occurs on a physical level when they coordinate their limbs and practice guiding them as a starting point for all further movement development. In later stages of life, this self-awareness is also transferred to the development of soul and spirit. If we allow children from the very beginning to discover the world and its laws themselves, we create the conditions for future independent learning. Basic trust and security are necessary prerequisites for the success of exploration – and must be disrupted as little as possible in the course of development. Experiencing the security of being in relationship is a prerequisite for later independence. Bonding and exploration cannot be done independently of each other.

The reciprocal dynamics of being together through bonding and being on one's own through exploration

In addition to the child's basic experiences of being together (bonding) and being on his own (exploration), there is another decisive element: the rhythm of alternating between the two poles, or the reciprocal dynamics. To study this, we mustestablish a new science of life forces. Life forces have a significant influence on lifelong health and regeneration. Here we must distinguish the physical body, which immediately begins to break down if it is not prevented from doing so by the vital forces, and the life forces themselves. Rudolf Steiner calls this function of life forces the etheric body.[8] Which laws underlie the life forces described here and how do they manifest? What promotes or inhibits them?

The unmistakable individuality of the child develops in the confrontation between what has become (the physical body), on the one hand, and the initially indeterminate persona on the other. In this area of tension we can perceive the forces of growth and well-being. As an example, this is comparable to the growth and decay of plants. In plants, a constant rhythm of contraction and expansion can be observed in the gesture of growth. This is repeated in a differentiated manner throughout the process from root formation to flowering. Plant growth is characterized by a rhythmic contraction and expansion. In other living examples, as in the human body, contraction and expansion are principles of vital forces. For example, we need only think of breathing—the intake of oxygen, the exhalation of carbon dioxide.

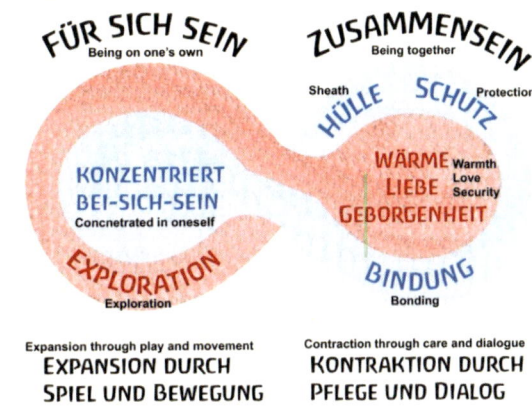

Diagram 4

Body formation and growth in the child's first seven years happen rhythmically and take place between two poles: day and night, waking and sleeping, playing and resting, being alone and being with others. It appears to be a fundamental characteristic of the life force that it is based on a rhythmic swinging between two poles, on a vibrant flowing back and forth. Yes, it is possible to recognize the health of an organism by the fact that this pendular movement and rhythm is pulsating and supple. Against the background of this description of the life forces, let us now consider the basic needs of commitment and exploration described at the beginning. Both poles, with their far-reaching psychological consequences, are mutually dependent on and transform each other.

In Diagram 4 the gestures of being together are on the right side of the drawing, depicted by the closedness of the protective cover (blue) and the heartiness of the warming child's soul (red). Being together allows the child to unfold her expanding interest in the world (left side) out of the concentration created in inner warming (right side).

Exploration thus creates autonomous self-development based on experiences of the world and increased sensory perception. The child retains her previously acquired "core" of centering and concentration (blue) to freely and creatively experience the world (red). Experiences of expansion in turn have an enhancing effect on the relationship of being together.

> "To truly know the world,
> look deeply within your own being;
> to truly know yourself, take real interest in the world."[9] Or:
> "Self-knowledge is rooted in world knowledge,
> World knowledge springs from self-knowledge."

The poles are mutually dependent. Each transforms itself while mirroring the other. Attachment theory, in which the significance of bonding for exploration has been extensively researched, is supplemented by the dynamics of the vital forces. This describes an important principle for promoting health in children. The application of this view can have a beneficial and practical effect on institutions for their concepts and in general for their consideration of children in pregnancy, childbirth, and through early childhood.

What are the consequences of this for education and therapy?

What conclusions can we draw for education and therapy from this observation of child development? What is needed for the vitality of the small child to develop optimally and thus become the basis for healthy physical development? From the foregoing discussion, it is apparent that, for small children, being together in care and being cared for (as a contractive gesture) should harmonize with the expansion of being on one's own in play and movement. This harmonizing and interdependent relationship between the elements of contraction and expansion can provide helpful answers to questions about salutogenesis and health.

If adults want to support the development of healthy vitality in their child, they must consciously adopt healthy attitudes – above all attentiveness towards the child and the ability to change their approach according to the situation. For example, the parent relates differently with the child when he or she is engaged in exploration, play and movement, compared with when the child is being cared for, put to bed, or comforted – thus when the focus is on relationship. There are different accompanying gestures we should adopt toward the child, always situational, and considering the perception of the child's needs. We might say:

- On the one hand, I support the child wherever he is dependent on me for something he cannot do for himself.
- On the other hand, I encourage all of his efforts towards independent and free development.

Parents and the environment as the basis of child development

The goals of child development, and the process of educating children to the point of maturity, are completely in accordance with the two observed basic phenomena – self-determination and the ability to be together in dialogue, to form healthy bonds and relationships. The basis for this – as we have already seen in the previous description of the archetypal phenomena – is the right environment. It includes not only basic needs such as food, shelter and provisions. Above all it requires an environment shaped by adults. The environment provides a framework and protection for the development of the basic soul needs of security, stability, and warmth, as well as for the spiritual needs of freedom, autonomy, and creativity. It is crucial – as we have seen – for all learning in relationships and independent learning.

Basic spiritual needs	Basic soul needs
Freedom	Security, safety
Autonomy	Bonding, Stability
Creativity	Trust, warmth, love
Independent learning	Learning in dialogue
Being on one's own	Being together
Basic physical needs such as food, shelter, care, protection	

The child's first environment

A child's first environment is always parents or other close reference persons, her adult role models. The younger the child, the more affected she will be by the attitudes lived by the adults around her; in older children it is the perceptible role model that has the strongest effect. What is the inner attitude of adults when dealing with children? Are they inwardly present or absent while they're with the children? Are they "genuine" or are they playing a role? Can they reflect on their own fears, needs, or even injuries, and regulate and steer these matters in a way that is responsive to children; can they perceive and be respectful of children's needs? All of this creates the basis for empathic togetherness, which is the scientific focus today even in neurobiology (mirror neurons).

In this respect, parents, teachers, and therapists who deal with children need the ability to constantly perceive themselves to be able to fulfill their role as reference persons. In professional life, self-education and self-governance must promote the therapeutic and artistic ability to support the pendulum movement between the two basic pillars of child development. This includes organizing one's own thoughts, directing one's feelings appropriately for the situation, and following with appropriate actions. For adults this process is like the steps leading up to a temple or altar: reflecting on one's own ideas (thinking), working through one's own feelings (feeling) and the resulting impulses for action (willing).

This attitude, as the first environment of the child, is particularly important in the early childhood years up to school readiness, in which the small child is above all connected with our mental and spiritual intentions. What image or question do we develop towards the child?

- Where have you come from?
- What are we creating together, what are we learning together, what is our relationship?
- Where will you go from here?

Thus the stream of the past meets with the developing future through the present environment formed by adults.

The parent, educator, or therapist who is educating and developing herself inwardly in her soul is confronted with a child who is growing in his physical organization. The dynamics of this relationship, through infinite repetitions of the gestures of being together and being on one's own (depending on age and development), form a life principle for long-term health. The child will grow into a person who depends on the self-regulation learned and applied in early childhood. With maturity, this pendulum play develops into the capacity for self-direction and self-education.

The environment and the specific approach depend on the different qualifications and tasks: pediatricians, doctors, and therapists can all make appropriate contributions to the child's health and to his ability to grasp his own biography by accepting his creative will.

Overview of the interaction between adults and children:

Adult	Child
Gives protection, creates form	Can test himself, play freely
Is reserved, waiting to see	Observes with concentration
Observes with concentration	becomes active, because he feels perceived
Is mindful, accompanying and reflecting	Can engage in concentrated activity
Is joyful and happy with the child	Is pleased about his activity and discovery
Is appreciative and empathetic	Is happy and relaxed

Incarnation in the picture of the temple

Since ancient times, the human body has been seen as a temple where the human spirit incarnates into individuality ("Or do you not know that your body is a temple of the Holy Spirit within you, whom you have from God? You are not your own." 1 Corinthians 6:19) If we summarize the developmental process of the small child, the two constantly shifting poles for the areas of independent learning and relationship learning form the "pillars" of the temple. The following keywords can be compiled for them:

Independent Learning	Relationship Learning
Free activity Being on one's own The child as a creator Movement, play	Caring for the child Being together The child as a relationship being Dialogical cooperation as needs are taken care of
Satisfying the need for: • Autonomy • Being independent • Creativity • Freedom • Meaning, etc..	Satisfying the need for: • Security • Trust • Warmth • Reliability • Safety, etc.
Role of the adult: Attentive perception of when the child needs support and when he wants to be undisturbed. Awake inwardly, active in observation, calm outwardly.	*Role of the adult:* The adult is a role model through her actions. Active outwardly, calm inwardly.
The child sets the impulses.	The child cooperates through: • Joining in • Helping • Trying things himself

The **basis** is the physical body inherited from his parents, with all of its predispositions and possibilities.

Surroundings

The environment plays an important role in the individualization process. The child's *first environment* is the adults and their attitude: presence, authenticity, appreciation and empathy – and working on developing these qualities – are the most important prerequisites for the effectiveness of education and the shaping of the personality.

The *second environment* is the physical-spatial environment as the outer framework.

This overview can be transferred to the following image of a temple (Diagram 5). The temple is an image for human development from the genetic material of the parents, within a concrete sociocultural environment, to an "I." The adult's capacity for self-determination and relationship – essential goals in all educational plans – are shown in the "architrave gallery of capacities." They are formed in the course of childhood and adolescence through the living gestures of independent learning and relationship learning in rhythmic, repetitive movements as prerequisites for the self-determining "I." The image of the temple stands for the development of the personality, just as every sacred building was and is a place in which the aspiring person could "straighten up" and change or realign himself.

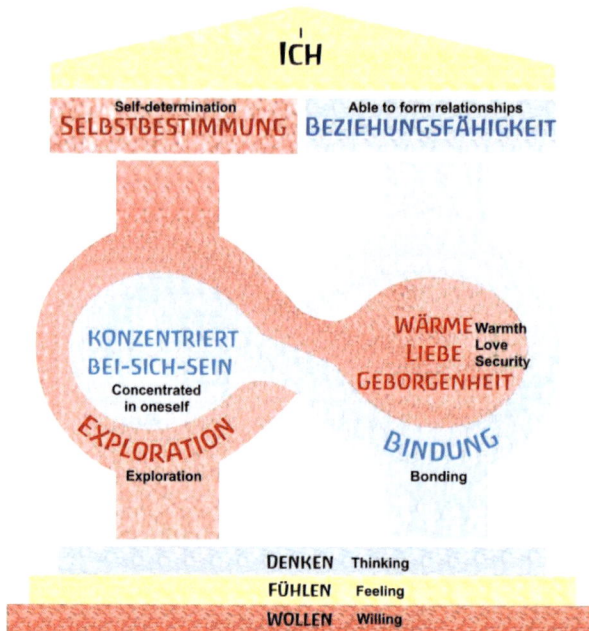

Diagram 5

Uprightness as a model of creation

All of early childhood development can be regarded as a process of the child erecting himself against gravity. In later stages of life there are similar experiences as soul and spiritual uprightness are achieved by the independent personality. The figure-eight phenomenon depicted in Diagram 6 arises from the configuration of the living, shape-forming life or etheric forces, characterized by the already described gestures of contraction and expansion. They are the builders of the physical body and the foundation for uprightness.

The more that the growth, structuring, and shaping of the organs are penetrated by the rhythm of activity, the more lasting the effect on lifelong health will be. The dynamics of the polar opposite forces of contraction and expansion are lively, flexible and supple. They are individually designed for each biography. It can be seen that these forces strive for balance and harmony, for example through the polarity of more internally oriented organs such as the heart, and more outwardly oriented organs such as the lungs. Just as the rhythm of the heart and lungs is decisive for human beings, both elements imprint themselves into the organ structure in early childhood: relationship (within) and exploration (without).

EDUCATIONAL FOUNDATIONS AND OBJECTIVES

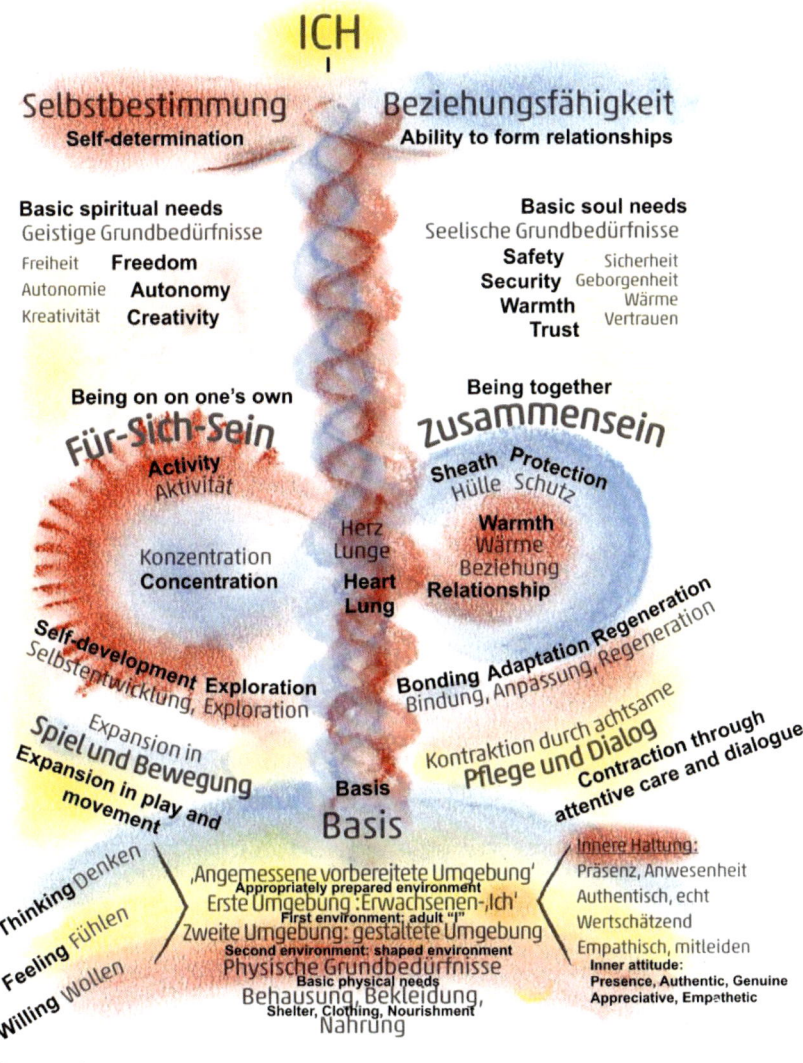

Diagram 6

These polarities are also apparent in the sex organs, female expressing inner space and male expressing radiance. These kinds of laws – curved and straight, contracting and expanding, left and right –also appear in Raphael's Sistine Madonna.

On the right, Saint Barbara stands with her gaze turned inward and her hands closed in front of her chest; on the left, Saint Sixtus stands with his right hand pointing and his gaze directed upward. The dynamics of bonding and exploration are embodied in these two figures. One can interpret Raphael's Sistine Madonna as an expression of human incarnation, observing the lively dynamic between the heavenly and earthly fields and the polarity of male creative will and female relational will. The main figure, the Madonna with Child, expresses on her right side by the way she holds the child:

You can go and become independent (exploration). I'll give you support, but I won't stop you.

On her left, or heart, side (with its red undergarment and protective veil):

I give you security, inner space and protection (bond).

Aren't all these relationships shown here exactly our mission to accompany children on their way through life? Here lie the common tasks and challenges of education, therapy and medicine for growing children and their parents. With this in mind, CARE 1, a project of the international Medical Section at the Goetheanum in Switzerland, works together as an interdisciplinary working group with a wide range of specialist skills and expertise in order to provide orientation for children and parents through a consistent view of the child's developing life.

---

1 Hüther, G., Gebauer, K. (2004) Kinder brauchen Wurzeln. Düsseldorf and Zurich: walter

2 Bauer, J. (2010) Das Gedächtnis des Körpers. Frankfurt: Piper

3 Schiffer, E., Schiffer, H. (2004) LernGesundheit: Lebensfreude und Lernfreude in der Schule und anderswo. Weinheim: Beltz

4 Winicott, D. (2018) Vom Spiel zur Kreativität. Stuttgart: Klett-Cotta

5 Grossmann, E.K., Grossmann, K. (2004) Bindungen: Das Gefüge psychischer Sicherheit. Stuttgart: Klett-Cotta

6 Steiner, R. (1969) Die gesunde Entwicklung des Leiblich-Physischen als Grundlage der freien entfaltung des Seelisch-Geistigen. In Gesamtausgabe 303, Dornach

7 Steiner, R. (1976) Die Erziehung des Kindes vom Gesichtspunkt der Geisteswissenschaft, Dornach

8 Steiner, R. (1953) Welterkenntnis Selbsterkenntnis.Wahrsprüche und Widmungen. Dornach

9 Steiner, R. (2004) Verses and Meditations. See, e.g., Verses and Meditations by Rudolf Steiner, translated by George Adams. Great Barrington: SteinerBooks

EDUCATIONAL FOUNDATIONS AND OBJECTIVES

Raphael, The Sistine Madonna, 1513-14
(Gemäldegalerie Alte Meister, Dresden).

Appendix: Quality criteria for day care centers with children under the age of three

Compiled by the Birth to Three Working Group (Arbeitskreis Kleinkind, *or* AKK) *that is part of the Association of Waldorf Kindergartens in Germany*

Society has seen far-reaching changes over the last years. These changes are due to factors such as the changed image of womanhood, the different relationships couples have now, the decreasing birthrate and the effect all these factors have on the work situation. Alongside this development, family structures have also changed drastically.

Waldorf teachers, together with anybody who carries responsibility for a school or center, need to find ways to guarantee the protection of childhood in the face of all these changes. In conferences that have taken place in the last ten years, the main concerns and tasks have been formulated. The conferences with the title "The Dignity of the Young Child" that took place in Dornach, Switzerland in 2000 and 2010 and in Järna, Sweden in 2004 had the aim of inspiring Waldorf schools and kindergartens to establish further training programs for educators and centers for very young children that are based on the anthroposophical view of the human being.

Because of their immense importance for an individual's entire life, the first three years need particular care and consideration. What young children need and what has been discovered by research into early child development needs to be taken into account and applied in practice.

The Birth to Three Working Group gave itself the task of developing quality criteria based on Rudolf Steiner's anthroposophy. These are intended as guidelines for the work with young children on the foundations of Waldorf education.

Creating a suitable environment

One of the guiding aspects of a center's educational concept is to create spaces and rhythms that best meet the essential developmental needs of young children. These include:

- **Security and attachment:** A reliable attachment figure, a careful settling-in process, transparent daily rhythms and routines, reliable spatial structures, time to cultivate the relationship in care situations. A special care area needs to be integrated into the main space to allow children to experience the meaningful care activities provided by the adults.
- **Exploring:** The environment, indoors as well as outdoors, must offer enough space and challenges for movement and play; there should be sufficient play materials that are inspiring, versatile and appropriate for the different ages.
- **Care for the foundational senses:** This applies to care products and food but also to the choice of toys, equipment and furnishings.
- **Experiences of the child's own impact on the environment:** The implementation of the above criteria allows children to experience their own impact on the world. Children need to be given ample opportunity, within the daily structure, to acquire autonomy and independence (by being actively involved in the care situation, during meals, etc.)

The Birth to Three Working Group, which is part of the German Association of Waldorf Kindergartens, considers it its task to establish criteria that can serve as conditions for good practice. Its members are teachers from training courses and birth-to-three educators who carry out research during their work meetings.

Basic training in Waldorf education

Depending on a country's legal requirements, a state-certified teaching qualification or a similar training is necessary. An additional qualification as Waldorf educator is desirable.

In every case, however, further anthroposophical training in early childhood education for children under the age of three is essential.

Staff requirements

- Familiarity with the anthroposophical view of the human being, including the development before birth and in the first three years.
- Biography work—an educator needs to look after her own physical and mental health. Professionalism in education can only be attained if educators strive for inner development.
- Willingness to cooperate with parents, colleagues, sponsors, regional institutions.
- Willingness to undergo supervision, peer review and "intervision" as well as continuous further training and in-service training.

Accepting children under the age of three

- The decision to accept children under the age of three needs the participation and approval of the entire teaching faculty and board, of a Waldorf kindergarten or school. In order to be successful, the undertaking needs to be carried and supported by the whole community.
- The importance of shared responsibility in this educational partnership needs to be part of the concept. This includes acceptance of each child's family situation.
- The center's ways of working need to be described in the concept.
- The settling-in period needs careful planning and is part of the center's concept.
- The significance of the attachment figure needs to be recognized by the center and included in plans for substitution (use of established, familiar substitute teachers).

Basic conditions for centers

Basic conditions have to include factors such as the educator-to-child ratio, group size and the qualification of staff members.

The time that educators need for preparation and review, for specialist and in-service training, also needs to be included, as does the center's equipment and materials and the continuous delivery of education and care.

National, state, provincial and local legal requirements also need to be taken into account.

Mixed-age groups, two to six years

- 15 children maximum, with a maximum of five children under the age of three. Educator-to-child ratio: 2:15, plus one intern or aide
- Age-appropriate program: the daily routine must be adjusted to the needs of the children at various developmental stages
- Room plan: sufficient space for younger and older children, separate areas that offer protected spaces for movement and play
- Diapering area in the part of the room that offers protection to the very young children, a room for sleeping, age-appropriate toys
- A settling-in procedure

If it is not possible to meet these conditions, then this kind of group is not recommended.

Groups with children age one to three
The above conditions apply, with these adjustments:
- 10 children maximum
- Educator-child ratio: 2:10, plus one aide
- Contact with the nursery/kindergarten is recommended in preparation for the transition.

Groups with children age birth to three
The same conditions apply, with these adjustments:
- 10 children maximum
- Educator-to-child ratio: 1:3, 1:4 maximum
- The recommended number of 10 children must not be exceeded. It has proved successful to separate the children into a group of birth-to-one-and-a-half and a group of one-and-a-half-to-three-year-olds.
- There should be a separate area for children who are not yet walking.

Advisory Service for founding new initiatives
The members of the Birth to Three Working Group offer an advisory service for founding initiatives in Germany. In collaboration with a school's teaching faculty, board, and parents, they develop a plan based on the needs of the children. All members of this working group are experienced in the institutional care of young children and are active in the training of birth-to-three educators.

THE CHILD FROM BIRTH TO THREE

English-language Resource List

See page 80 for the bibliography from the German edition, to which all citations in the main text refer. This list includes titles from the German bibliography that are available in English, as well as additional suggested resources.

Ainsworth, M. D. S., M.C. Blehar, E. Waters, E., and S. Wall. *Patterns of Attachment: A psychological study of the strange situation*. Hillsdale, NJ: Erlbaum, 1978.

Aldinger, Cynthia and Mary O'Connell. *Home Away from Home*. Oklahoma: LifeWays North America, 2010.

Antonovsky, A. *Health, Stress and Coping*. San Francisco: Jossey-Bass, 1979.

————— *Unraveling The Mystery of Health: How People Manage Stress and Stay Well*. San Francisco: Jossey-Bass, 1987.

Baldwin, Rahima. *You Are Your Child's First Teacher*. Berkeley: Celestial Arts, 1989.

Baldwin, Sarah. *Nurturing Children and Families: One Model of a Parent-Child Program in a Waldorf School*. Spring Valley: WECAN Books, 2004.

Bauer, Dietrich, Max Hoffmeister, and Hartmut Goerg. *Children Who Communicate Before They are Born*. Forest Row, UK: Temple Lodge, 2005.

Biddulph, Steve. *Raising Babies: Should under-threes go to nursery?* London, UK: Thorsons, 2006.

Blom, Ria. *Crying and Restlessness in Babies*. Edinburgh, UK: Floris Books, 2003.

Bowlby, John. *The Making and Breaking of Affectional Bonds*. London: Routledge, 1979.

Brazelton, T. Berry, and Stanley Greenspan. *The Irreducible Needs of Children: What every child must have to grow, learn and flourish*. New York: Da Capo, 2011.

Brisch, Karl-Heinz. *Treating Attachment Disorders: From Theory to Therapy*. New York: The Guilford Press, 2004.

Brownlee, Pennie. *Dance with Me in the Heart: the Adult's Guide to Great Infant-Parent Relationships*. New Zealand: Playcentre Publications, 2008.

Clouder, Christopher, and Janni Nichol. *Creative Play for Your Baby*. London, UK: Gaia Books, 2008.

Doidge, Norman. *The Brain that Changes Itself: Stories of Personal Triumph from the Frontiers of Brain Science*. New York: Penguin, 2007.

Drake, Stanley. *The Path to Birth*. Edinburgh, UK: Floris, 1979.

Eliot, Lise. *What's Going On in There? How the brain and mind develop in the first five years of life*. New York: Bantam, 2000.

Ellersiek, Wilma. *Giving Love – Bringing Joy*. Spring Valley: WECAN Books, 2003.

Gerber, Magda. *Your Self-Confident Baby*. New York: John Wiley, 1998.

——— *Dear Parent*. Los Angeles: RIE, 1999.

Glas, Norbert. *Conception, Birth, and Early Childhood*. Spring Valley: Anthroposophic Press, 1983.

Glöckler, Michaela, ed. *The Dignity of the Young Child: Care and training for the first three years of life*. Dornach, Switzerland: Medical Section at the Goetheanum, 1999.

Glöckler, Michaela, and Wolfgang Goebel. *A Guide to Child Health*. Edinburgh, UK: Floris Books, 1990.

Goddard, Sally. *What Babies and Children Really Need*. Stroud, UK: Hawthorn Press, 2008.

Gonzalez-Mena, Janet and Dianne Widmeyer Eyer. *Infants, Toddlers, and Caregivers: A curriculum of respectful, responsive care and education*, eighth edition. Columbus: McGraw Hill, 2008.

Grossmann, Klaus E., Karin Grossmann and Everett Waters, eds. *Attachment from Infancy to Adulthood: The Major Longitudinal Studies*. New York: Guildford, 2006.

Heckmann, Helle. *Nøkken: A Garden for Children*. Spring Valley: WECAN Books, no date.

——— *Childhood's Garden: Shaping Everyday Life Around the Needs of Young Children*. Spring Valley: WECAN Books, 2008

Hermsen-van Waanroy, Marianne. *Babymoves*. New Zealand: Babymoves Publications, 2002.

Howard, Susan, ed. *The Developing Child: The First Seven Years*. Spring Valley: WECAN Books, 2004.

Hüther, Gerald. *The Compassionate Brain: How Empathy Creates Intelligence*. Boston: Trumpeter, 2006.

Kallo, Eva and Gyorgyi Balog. *The Origins of Free Play*. Budapest: Pikler-Loczy Tarsasag, 2005.

Kitzinger, Sheila and Lennart Nilsson. *Being Born*. New York: Grosset and Dunlap, 1986.

König, Karl. *Eternal Childhood*. Botton Village, UK: Camphill Press, 1994.

——— *The First Three Years of the Child*. New York: Anthroposophic Press, 1969.

Odent, Michel. *Primal Health: understanding the critical period between conception and the first birthday*. Forest Row, UK: Clairview, 2002.

Patterson, Barbara. *Beyond the Rainbow Bridge*. Amesbury: Michaelmas Press, 2000.

Patzlaff, Rainer. *Childhood Falls Silent*. Forest Row, UK: Steiner Waldorf Schools Fellowship.

Piaget, Jean and Barbel Inhelder. *The Psychology of the Child*. New York: Basic Books, 1972.

Pikler, Emmi. *Peaceful Babies, Contented Mothers*, sixth edition. Budapest:Medicina,1963.

Pikler Institute. *Unfolding of infants' natural gross motor development*. Los Angeles: RIE, 2006.

Raichle, Bernadette. *Creating a Home for Body, Soul and Spirit: A new approach to child care*. Spring Valley: WECAN Books, 2008.

Ris, Margaret and Trice Atchison, eds. *A Warm and Gentle Welcome: Nurturing Children from Birth to Age Three*. Spring Valley: WECAN Books, 2008.

Roche, Mary Alice, ed. *Emmi Pikler 1902-1984*. Sensory Awareness Foundation Bulletin #14, Winter 1994. Mill Valley, CA: Sensory Awareness Foundation, 1994.

Rohen, Johannes. *Functional Morphology: The Dynamic Wholeness of the Human Organism*. Ghent: Adonis Press, 2007.

Salter, Joan. *The Incarnating Child*. Stroud, UK: Hawthorn Press, 1987.

——— *Mothering With Soul*. Stroud, UK: Hawthorn Press, 1998.

Soesman, Albert. *Our Twelve Senses*. Stroud, UK: Hawthorn Press, 1999.

Steiner, Rudolf. *Prayers for Parents and Children*. London, UK: Rudolf Steiner Press, 1983.

——— *The Spiritual Guidance of the Individual and Humanity*. Hudson: Anthroposophic Press, 1992.

——— "The Education of the Child in the Light of Spiritual Science" in *The Education of the Child and Early Lectures on Education*. (Hudson, Anthroposophic Press, 1996

——— "The Child Before the Seventh Year" in *Soul Economy and Waldorf Education*. Hudson: Anthroposophic Press, 1986.

——— *Understanding Young Children: Excerpts from Lectures by Rudolf Steiner*. Spring Valley: WECAN Books, 1994.

Udo de Haes, Daniel. *The Young Child: Creative living with two to four-year-olds*. Spring Valley, NY: Anthroposophic Press, 1986.

Bibliography from the German Edition

Please see page 77 for a list of English-language resources, including titles on this list that have been translated into or were originally published in English.

Ainsworth, M.D. / Blehar, M.C. / Waters, E. / Wall, S. (1978): Patterns of Attachment A psychological Study of the Strange Situation. New York

Antonovsky, Aaron (1993): Gesundheitsforschung versus Krankheitsforschung. in: A. Franke / M. Broda (Hrsg.): Psychosomatische Gesundheit. Tübingen. S.3–14

Antonovsky, Aaron (1997): Salutogenese. Zur Entmystifvzierung der Gesundheit. Deutsche erweiterte Herausgabe von A. Franke. Tübingen

Auer, Wolfgang M. (2007): Sinneswelten. Die Sinne entwickeln, Wahrnehmung schulen, mit Freude lernen. München

Bauer, Joachim (2005): Warum ich fühle, was du fühlst. Hamburg

Biddulph, Steve (2007): Das Geheimnis glücklicher Babys. Kinderbetreung – ab wann, wie oft, wie lange? München

Blom, Ria / Charpey, Thomas / Barendrecht, Susanne (2005): Wenn Babys häufi geschreien – Wirksame Hilfe durch Rhythmus und Pucken. Stuttgart

Bowlby, John / Ainsworth, Mary D. (Hrsg.) (1966): Deprivation of Maternal Care. New York

Brisch, Karl-Heinz / Grossmann, Klaus E. / Grossmann, Karin / Köhler, Lotte (Hrsg.) (2006): Bindung und seelische Entwicklungswege. Grundlagen, Prävention und klinische Praxis. Stuttgart, 2. Auflage

Brisch, Karl-Heinz / Hellbrügge, Theodor (Hrsg.) (2008): Der Säugling – Bindung, Neurobiologie und Gene. Stuttgart

Doidge, Norman (2007): The Brain That Changes Itself. New York, Viking. Deutsch:Neustart im Kopf: Wie sich unser Gehirn selbst repariert. Übersetzung von Jürgen Neubauer.

Campus-Verlag, Frankfurt a. M. & New York 2008, ISBN 978-3-593-38534-1 Dornes, Martin (2006): Die Seele des Kindes – Entstehung und Entwicklung. Frankfurt/Main

Dornes, Martin (2009): Der kompetente Säugling. Frankfurt/Main, 14. Auflage

Eliot, Lise (2001): Was geht da drinnen vor? Die Gehirnentwicklung in den ersten fünf Lebensjahren (Deutsche Übersetzung). Berlin

Fels, Nicola / Knabe, Angelika / Maris, Bartholomeus (2003): Ins Leben begleiten. Schwangerschaft und erstes Lebensjahr. Stutgart

Gebauer, Karl / Hüther, Gerald (2005): Kinder brauchen Wurzeln. Neue Perspektiven für eine gelingende Erziehung. Düsseldorf/Zürich

Göbel, Wolfgang / Glöckler, Michaela (2010): Kindersprechstunde. Ein medizinischpädagogischer Ratgeber. Stuttgart, 18. Auflage

Gonzalez Mena, Janet / Widmeyer Eyer, Dianne (2008): Säuglinge, Kleinkinder und ihre Betreuung, Erziehung und Pflege. Freiamt

Grah-Wittich, Claudia (2007): Quasselliese und Zappelphilipp. in: Neider, Andreas (Hrsg.) Brauchen Jungen eine andere Erziehung als Mädchen? Stuttgart

Grossarth-Maticek, Ronald (1999): Systemische Epidemiologie und präventive Verhaltensmedizin chronischer Erkrankungen. Strategien zur Aufrechterhaltung der Gesundheit. Berlin / New York

Grossmann, K.E. & Grossmann, K. (Hrsg.) (2003). Bindung und menschliche Entwicklung.

John Bowlby, Mary Ainsworth und die Grundlagen der Bindungstheorie und Forschung. Stuttgart

Hengstenberg, Elfriede (2002): Entfaltungen. Bilder und Schilderungen aus meiner Arbeit mit Kindern. Emmendingen, 3. Auflage

Hüther, Gerald (2001): Bedienungsanleitung für ein menschliches Gehirn. Göttingen, 2. Auflage

Hüther, Gerald (2002): Wohin? Wofür? Weshalb? Über die Bedeutung innerer Leitbilder für die Hirnentwicklung. in: Gebauer / Hüther (Hrg.) Kinder suchen Orientierung. Anregungen für eine sinn-stiftende Erziehung. Düsseldorf / Zürich

Hüther, Gerald / Krens, Inge (2003): Das Geheimnis der erste drei Monate. Unsere frühesten Prägungen. Düsseldorf, 2. Auflage

König, Karl (2003): Die ersten drei Jahres des Kindes. Stuttgart, 3. Auflage

Kutik, Christiane (2007): Entscheidende Kinderjahre. Ein Handbuch zur Erziehung von 0 bis 7. Stuttgart, 3. Auflage

Largo, Remo H. (2010): Babyjahre. Entwicklung und Erziehung in den ersten vier Jahren. Völlig überarbeitete Neuausgabe München

Largo, Remo (2004): Kinderjahre. Die Individualität des Kindes als erzieherische

Herausforderung. München, 9. Auflage

Leber, Stefan (1996): Der Schlaf und seine Bedeutung. Geisteswissenschaftliche Dimensionen des Un- und Überbewussten. Stuttgart

Oerter, Rolf / Montada, Leo (Hrsg.) (2002): Entwicklungspsychologie. Weinheim, Basel, Berlin. 5. Auflage

Opp, Günther / Fingerle, Michael / Freytag, Andreas (Hrsg.) (1999): Was Kinder stärkt. Erziehung zwischen Risiko und Resilienz. München / Basel

Patzlaff, Rainer (2004): Der gefrorene Blick. Physiologische Wirkungen des Fernsehens und die Entwicklung des Kindes. Stuttgart, 3. Auflage

Piaget, Jean / Inhelder, B. (1973): Die Psychologie des Kindes. Olten

Pikler, Emmi (1982): Friedliche Babys – zufriedene Mütter. Pädagogische Ratschläge einer Kinderärztin. Freiburg/Basel/Wien, 11.Auflage

Pikler, Emmi (2001): Lasst mir Zeit. Die selbständige Bewegungsentwicklung des Kindes bis zum freien Stehen. München, 3. Auflage

Pikler, Emmi (2002): Miteinander vertraut werden. Erfahrungen und Gedanken zur Pflege von Säuglingen und Kleinkindern. Freiamt, 3. Auflage

Raichle, Bernadette (2008): Creating a Home for Body, Soul and Spirit. A New Approach to Childcare. Waldorf Early Childhood Association of North America. Spring Valley

Grah-Wittich, Claudia (2008): Autonomes Lernen von Anfang an. in: Neider, Andreas (Hrsg.) Autonom lernen – intuitiv verstehen. Stuttgart

Riemann, Ilka / Wüstenberg, Wiebke (2004): Die Kindergartengruppe für Kinder ab einem Jahr öffnen? Eine empirische Studie. Fachhochschulverlag Frankfurt/Main

Rittelmeyer, Christian (1994): Schulbauten positiv gestalten. Wie Schüler Farben und Formen erleben. Wiesbaden / Berlin

Rittelmeyer, Christian (2002): Pädagogische Anthropologie des Leibes. Biologische Voraussetzungen der Erziehung und Bildung. Weinheim / München

Rohen, Johannes (2002): Morphologie des menschlichen Organismus. Stuttgart, 2. Auflage

Saßmannshausen, Wolfgang (2003): Waldorfpädagogik im Kindergarten. Freiburg / Brsg.

Schad, Wolfgang (2004): Die Idee der Evolution in der Pädagogik. in: Erziehungskunst 9 / 2004, S. 931–942

Schäfer, Gerd E. (Hrsg.) (2004): Bildung beginnt mit der Geburt. Ein offener

Bildungsplan für Kindertageseinrichtungen in Nordrhein-Westfalen. Weinheim / Basel, 2. Auflage

Schüffel, Wolfram et alii (Hrsg.) (1998): Handbuch der Salutogenese. Konzept und Praxis. Wiesbaden

Spitzer, Manfred (2002): Lernen. Gehirnforschung und die Schule des Lebens. Heidelberg/Berlin

Steiner, Rudolf (1907): Die Erziehung des Kindes vom Gesichtspunkte der Geisteswissenschaft. Dornach 2003

Steiner, Rudolf (1911): Die geistige Führung des Menschen und der Menschheit. Dornach

Steiner, Rudolf (1922): Die gesunde Entwickelung des Menschenwesens. Eine Einführung in die anthroposophische Pädagogik und Didaktik. 16 Vorträge. Dornach 4. Auflage 1987

Strub, Ute / Tardos, Anna (Hrsg.) (2006): Im Dialog mit dem Säugling. Pikler Gesellschaft Berlin

Vincze, Maria (1992): Schritte zum selbständigen Essen. Pikler-Gesellschaft Berlin

Zimmer, Renate (2004): Handbuch der Bewegungserziehung. Grundlagen für Ausbildung und pädagogische Praxis. Freiburg/Basel/Wien 18. Auflage

Zimmer, Renate / Hunger, Ina (Hrsg.) (2004): Wahrnehmen, Bewegen, Lernen. Kindheit in Bewegung. Schorndorf

About the Authors

Claudia Grah-Wittich is a qualified social pedagogue, working as educational adviser and early learning specialist at der hof, an education center in Frankfurt-Niederursel/Germany. She is also a lecturer on early childhood education.

Ina von Mackensen is an early childhood educator at the day nursery Wiegestube and a lecturer at the Waldorf Kindergarten Seminar, both in Berlin/Germany.

Claudia McKeen, MD is a general practitioner and school and kindergarten doctor. She is also a lecturer at the Waldorf Kindergarten Seminar in Stuttgart/Germany.

Rainer Patzlaff, PhD is professor of childhood education at Alanus Independent University in Alfter near Bonn/Germany and director of the IPSUM Institute in Stuttgart/Germany.